CHINESE

ARTISTIC

KITES

CHINESE ARTISTIC KITES

By Ha Kuiming and Ha Yiqi

Photography by Wang Xu

Translated by Ralph Kiggell

Chief Editor:	Chen Wanxiong
Executive Editor:	Guan Peizhen
Arts Coordinators:	Wen Yisha and You Bishan
Designer:	Wu Yuying
Photographer:	Wang Xu
Cover and text design for North American Edition:	Robbin Henderson

Copyright © 1990 by the Commercial Press, Ltd., Hong Kong. All rights reserved.
Original Chinese edition published in 1986 by The Commercial Press, Ltd., Hong Kong.

North American edition first published in 1990 by China Books & Periodicals, Inc.
Printed in Hong Kong by C & C Joint Printing Co.

Library of Congress Catalog Card Number: 89-60883
ISBN 0-8351-2279-4

FORWARD

Kites originated in China and were popular as a folk craft there long before spreading across the world. For four generations, the Ha family has been making kites, exploring new techniques, absorbing the best features of other kites into our designs and continuously adapting and creating to form a unique style. This book presents, for the first time in print, the results of our experiences and experiments and we hope it will encourage the traditional craft of kite-making.

This volume is based on actual practice with reference to the special characteristics of Chinese and foreign kites. It shows our individual developments and the more traditional theories and practices of kite design and construction.

Realizing that no single work could fully discuss the artistic theory and constructon of all Ha kites, we have attempted to provide the best possible introduction, one which will enable the reader both to appreciate the aesthetic of kites and to learn the practical construction techniques.

The Authors

Table of Contents

6

List of Illustrations
COLOR PLATES

7

FIGURES

Chapter 1

A Brief History Of Chinese Kites

Kite-making as a craft began in China thousands of years ago and spread very early to Korea, Japan and Southeast Asia, reaching the Middle East and Europe by the ninth century. Indeed, the British scholar Joseph Needham, in his *Science and Civilization in China,* contends that the kite was one of the most important scientific devices to have come to Europe from China.

The aerodynamic principles of kite-flying were a major factor in the development of aviation. In 1903, the Americans Wilbur Wright (1867–1912) and his younger brother Orville (1871–1948) carried out successive experiments with kites before building the frame of their airplane. With the addition of propelling machinery they could prolong the period of time the invention remained airborne. And everyone knows how Benjamin Franklin used a kite in his famous experiment demonstrating that lightning was a form of electricity.

The exact year and place where kites originated in China is not known, but probably the first recorded mention of kites was some 2500 years ago during the Spring and Autumn Period (722–481 B.C.). Gong Shuban, the founder of carpentry, who lived in the State of Lu, made a kite which imitated the form of sparrow hawks circling in the sky. But the earliest function of kites appears to have been military. The kite was used by the Lu army to spy on the enemy capital of the Song State.

Another story claims that the philosopher Mozi took three years to construct a wooden kite. Legend has it that during the warring between the states of Chu and Han (206–202 B.C.), Han Xin, a famous general, flew a wooden kite and used the length of the string to determine his distance from the enemy's palace. Having ascertained the position, a tunnel was dug and the palace duly attacked. During the same period (202 B.C.), he surrounded the Chu force led by the famous General Xiang Yu and devised a plan to rout the enemy. He spent day and night constructing a giant wooden kite for the great warrior, Zhang Liang, to ride in. Zhang Liang flew above the Chu encampment singing Chu songs. Hearing the songs, the soldiers were so saddened with thoughts of home that they dispersed and Xiang Yu was defeated.

With the invention of paper by Cai Lun (A.D.105), wood was no longer used to make kites. According to historical records, however, kites continued to be employed for military purposes right up until the Jin and Yuan dynasties (1115–1368). During the reign of the Southern Dynasties (420–589), the general leading rebel forces of the State of Liang in 543, surrounded the Emperor of Liang in his palace. The Emperor's son made a paper kite which flew high enough to notify distant allies of their plight. A similar record tells how, toward the end of the Tang Dynasty, the rebel general

Tian Yue, surrounded the city of Linming in 782 and the besieged general, Zhang Pi, used a paper kite to summon help. Again, in the Jin and Yuan dynasties, when the Yuan general, Su Bu, attacked the capital of the Jin in 1232, kites were used for the same purpose. In the Ming Dynasty (1368–1644), a kind of flying device called "sacred fire crow" could carry explosives to attack an enemy (fig. 5).

Near the beginning of the Tang Dynasty (618–907), the kite also came to be used more for pure enjoyment. During the Five Dynasties (907–960), Li Ye made a kite in the palace and fixed bamboo pipes to the head so that they would make a sound in the wind like the *zheng,* a stringed instrument. Ever since then, the word for kite in Chinese has been *fengzheng.* Most kites of that time were made of silk painted with gorgeous designs and carrying ornate accessories. The costliness of the kites suggests that they were playthings exclusively for the royalty and aristocracy. Not until the Northern Song (960–1127) did kites gradually become a more popular and common amusement. During the Southern Song (1127–1279), the first widely celebrated kite-fliers brought kites into special prominence.

During its development, kite-flying became a seasonal activity. Fuchadunchong of the late Qing Dynasty period wrote in his *Annual Records of the Seasons in Yanjing* (Beijing): "Children's play varies according to the seasons. After the tenth month there are kites and shuttlecocks and so on. Kites *(fengzheng)* and paper kites *(zhiyuan)* have bamboo frames and when fixed together, they make red-crowned cranes, peacocks, geese, flying tigers and the like and all are painted superbly. When the children fly them, they are extremely eye-catching. The modulating tone of those that carry a hummer or a gong and drum can be heard."

Today, techniques and designs are even more sophisticated, but kite-making is increasingly appreciated by millions.

Because kite-making and flying are traditional folk crafts, they naturally have a strong popular flavor and are closely related to folk customs. Every year in October, kite enthusiasts seem to wake from hibernation. The three months from Chinese New Year (usually in January and February) through *Qingming* (usually in March or April), comprise the main kite-flying season because of favorable winds. The sky above wide squares and open spaces fills with color and beauty, dazzling the spectators. But as soon as Qingming has passed, few kites are seen, as kite flying is halted by the great clouds of yellow dust blown down from the deserts north of Beijing.

In the past, many popular superstitions were related to kite-flying. One belief was that if the kite string broke and the kite drifted into someone's house, it was a bad

1. **Traditional Chinese kites** (1).

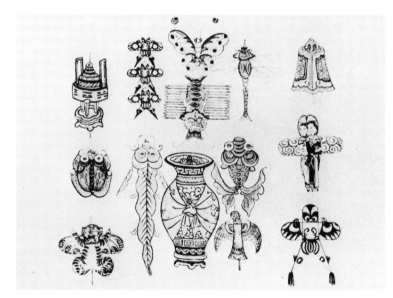

2. **Traditional Chinese kites** (2).

3. Children playing with kites

4. ("A Good Spring Wind," by Gao Yinzhang, late Qing Dynasty).

omen and the kite would have to be destroyed to avert misfortune. If the kite fell into the courtyard of a neighboring house, the kite owner could attempt to reclaim it. The neighbor might reluctantly return it after punching two holes in the kite's surface to dispel bad luck.

People in North China also believed that during the Lantern Festival (the fifteenth day of the first month in the Chinese calendar), every household must send the God of Wealth, who descended on New Year's Eve, back to heaven. Therefore, everyone from the poorest peasant to the richest prince went out at midday to fly kites. When night came, kites continued to fly, after people tethered the strings and went inside. At midnight, there would be more excitement as everybody would come out again to tie lanterns to the kite strings and set off firecrackers. After midnight, the God of Wealth was usually assumed to have returned to heaven and the

5. **A Ming Dynasty weapon,** "sacred fire crow."

此中國放風箏之圖也每到春季無事之人
用竹披子做成蝴蝶亥各樣飛禽不等上繫
線一條望空放起人仰面視之以吸空氣所謂
衛生也

6. **Flying a kite.** One Hundred Pictures of Beijing Folk Customs.

16

celebrants would go home to sleep, leaving the kites still flying. In the morning, the kites would have disappeared, leaving only some string behind. It was believed that the kite took trouble and disaster away with it.

The design of the kite's frame and the motifs it carried were also examples of folk superstition. For example, one of the rigid-wing Sand Swallow kites called the "slim swallow" has a thin, long frame and an overall graceful, "feminine" design. The "wide swallow," on the other hand, is broad and sturdy with a "masculine" design. A double swallow could be made by combining the slim and the wide swallow together to represent marital unity. Even "baby" swallow kites have been made. The designs on the kites are very closely related to traditional folk designs. They are never purely decorative but all have some special meaning. Some illustrate a plot from a folk tale or historical legend, while others carry a design with auspicious import such as Chang E, who became moon goddess, Zheng Chenggong, a famous general who recovered Taiwan, or the characters meaning "Great Prosperity Fills the Sky." (plates 63, 74 and 90).

Although making and flying kites requires care and skill, it is a hobby that can be enjoyed by everyone. While basic principles of aerodynamics must be followed to insure flight, there are no absolute rules of design, and people may develop their own methods of binding, gluing and decoration according to their own experience and tastes.

References

Joseph Needham, *Science and Civilization in China,* Trans., The Translation Group (Hong Kong: Zhong Hua Book Co., 1975), vol. 1, p. 548.

Duan Chengshi (Tang Dynasty), "Bianwu," in *Youyang zazu xuji,* (Beijing: Zhong Hua Book Co., 1981), pp. 233–234.

"Zuoshang Waichushuo," see *Han Feizi* (Shanghai: Zhong Hua Book Co., 1965), p. 184.

Gao Cheng (Song Dynasty), *Shiwu Jiyuan,* (*Records of Things*) (Taibei: Taiwan Commercial Printing Press, [n.d., 1982]), p. 34.

Zhao Xin (Tang Dynasty), *Xidengyaowen* (*Collections of Ancient and Modern Paintings*) (Shanghai: Zhong Hua Book Co., 1934), vol. 487, p. 36.

Li Kang (Tang Dynasty), *Duyizhi* (Shanghai: Commercial Press, 1937), p. 23.

Ouyang Xiu and Song Qi (Song Dynasty), "Tianyuezhuan," in *Xintangshu* (*New History of the Tang Dynasty*), (Beijing: Zhong Hua Book Co., 1975), vol. 19, p. 5928.

Bi Yuan (Qing Dynasty), *Xuzizhitongjian* (*Continuation of History as a Mirror*), (Beijing: Zhong Hua Book Co., 1964), vol. 166, p. 4519.

Chen Yi (Ming Dynasty), *Xunchulu* (Taibei: Taiwan Commercial Printing Press, 1969), p.3.

Fuchadunchong (Qing Dynasty), *Annual Records of the Seasons in Yanjing* ,(Beijing: Beijing Ancient Books Publishing House, 1981), p. 85.

Li Shi (Song Dynasty), *Xubowuzhi* (Taibei: Taiwan Commercial Printing Press, 1969), vol. 10, p. 7.

Chapter 2 The Evolution and Basic Structure of Ha Family Kites

The Ha family were originally builders, but because of the seasonal nature of construction, they turned to kite-making as a sideline in the mid-nineteenth century. Now, a hundred years later, they have evolved into an important kite-making school in China, where many different schools continue the long tradition.

The first member of the family to start making kites was Ha Guoliang. He was passionately interested in kites and, after studying them carefully and gradually amassing knowledge based on continuous experimentation, he was able to lay down the basic rules of construction.

Ha Guoliang's son, Ha Changying, continued the new family profession. By studying his father's craft assiduously, spending hours in parks exploring every nook and cranny, and observing every form of animal life to be found there, he gradually built up a store of material while developing an artistic awareness that gave his kites a distinctive style. Ha Changying not only created many forms of kites, but also designed some massive kites. In 1920, he constructed a 26-foot-long rigid-wing flower basket kite (wingspan is the measure of size for rigid-wing kites), the largest Ha kite ever developed. He also recorded specific guidelines, measurements and dimensions for every kite form he made, regardless of size. It is primarily due to his effort and creativity that the kites of this school have a distinctive style. In 1915, Ha Changying's reputation grew when he won a silver medal and certificate of merit for his Butterfly, Frog, Phoenix and Red-crowned Crane kites at the Panama International Fair held in California.

The third generation consists of the sons and daughters of Ha Changying. Each of the five children of Ha Changying has played an important role in continuing and developing the family tradition. The eldest son, Ha Kuibin, is particularly adept at kite construction; the second and third sons, Ha Kuishou and Ha Kuiliang, have concentrated on flying technique; the daughter, Ha Jingyi, often assists in kite-making and flying, and the fourth son, Ha Kuiming, is involved in all aspects of kite-craft. He continued the family tradition during difficult times, passing on the craft to his son, Ha Yiqi. (figs. 7–ll).

In recent years, Ha family kites have been exhibited and admired, not only in China, but in England, the United States, France, Japan, Canada, West Germany, India, Sweden and in Southeast Asia. In 1983 and 1984, when Ha Yiqi demonstrated kite-making and kite flying at various international meetings such as the San Francisco International Kite Festival, he touched off a worldwide interest in Chinese kites (figs. 12–19).

7. **The third generation of Has**. From left to right, Kuishou, Kuiliang and co-author, Kuiming.

9. **Ha Kuiming painting kite cover**.

8. **Ha Kuiming binding kite frame.**

10. **Ha Kuiming explains construction of kite to his son**, Yiqi (left) and students.

11. **Lecturing on kite construction**, Children's Palace, Beijing, 1982.

12. **Ha Yiqi with members of the American Kite Association** during a 1983 visit to the United States to lecture on kite construction techniques.

13. **Ha Yiqi with students** who have made double-flag kites after his lecture at the China Cultural Center of America in 1983.

14. **Ha Yiqi demonstrating kite-flying.** In 1983, he flew a 160-foot dragon-headed centipede at the San Francisco International Kite Festival.

15. **About to launch kite.**

16. **Ha Yiqi with some Ha family kites** now in the collection of the Pacific Science Center, 1984.

17. **Teaching kite-making techniques** at the Pacific Science Center, 1984.

Certificate of Achievement

presented to

Master Ha

for

his valuable contribution at the San Francisco International Kite Festival~1983~

18. **Certificate of Achieve ment** awarded at the San Francisco Kite Festival.

19. **Cup award.**

Various Ha kites, both old and new, can now be seen in the collections of many museums, both Chinese and foreign. For example, the Pacific Science Center in Seattle has exhibited four Ha kites; a Double Fish, a Zhong Kui Figure kite, a Gourd-shaped kite with lotus and a Cooking Pot. (figs. 20–23). The Bibliotheque Nationale in France has a Dragon-headed Centipede kite; the National Museum of Japan has two Slim Sand Swallow kites; and the Cultural Palace of Nationalities in China has more than ten different types of Ha family kites. It is not known exactly how many are in private collections (fig. 24).

The size of the Ha kites ranges from huge dimensions down to kites as tiny as 4" x 2 3/4". The largest kite made recently spans 23 feet (figs. 25–26). In the construction of the different kites, the exact design specifications and procedures for assembly are strictly adhered to.

On the basis of frame, coordinating design, flying performance and wind resistance, Chinese kites are classified into eight major types: rigid-wing, flexible wing, rigid square-frame, flexible square-frame, soft flap, multiple-layered, umbrella wing and three dimensional.

These categories correspond to different levels of wind resistance required because of variations in wind speed. An example of this is the great difference in wind resistance between the rigid-wing and the flexible-wing kite, mainly due to the difference in wing construction. The top and bottom edges of the rigid wing kite are supported with bamboo struts and the paper or silk is glued to this to create a wind-resisting surface. By contrast, only the top edge of the wing of the flexible-wing kite is supported with bamboo, leaving the bottom edge unsupported, thus reducing its wind resistance.

In a strong wind, up to 60 percent of the air current will pass under the unsupported bottom edge of the wing and, because of the gravitational force, the kite's lifting power will be badly affected, or at worst, the kite will somersault and even fall. But owing to its larger wind-resisting surface, the rigid-wing kite is able to fly well in high winds. If the wind is not strong, then only about 40 percent of the air current will pass under the unsupported edge of the flexible-wing kite, the gravitational force and lifting power will be even and its flight will be much steadier.

Among the eight major kite types, the following are a few of the many finely divided variations based on construction, decoration and theme.

20. **Double Fish.**

21. **Zhong Kui.**

22. **Gourd-Shaped kite with lotus.**

23. **Cooking Pot.**

24. **Kite purchased for private American collection.** This 80-inch Phoenix kite was purchased for $870.

25. **Flower Basket with 23 foot breadth.**

26. **Wide Swallow kite only 2 3/4 inches wide.**

1. Rigid-wing types. The upper and lower wing edges are all defined with bamboo (fig. 27). There are three basic types:

1) Sand swallow. This includes the Slim Sand Swallow (fig. 28; plates 1–4) and the Wide Sand Swallow (fig. 29; plates 6–9).

2) Asterisk frame. This is the frame for several designs including the human figure, birds, animals and insects, etc. (fig.30; plates 11–14; 16–18; 20). In Chinese this is called the rice-character frame because it resembles the character for rice.

3) Multi-layered. Ranging from two to several layers, the designs include frogs, insects, single Chinese characters, multiple Chinese characters, pagoda shapes, etc. (figs. 31–33; plates 21–24).

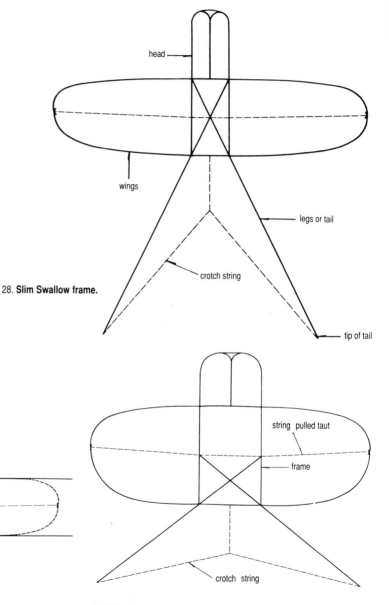

28. **Slim Swallow frame.**

27. **Wing frame of rigid-wing kite.**

29. **Wide Swallow frame.**

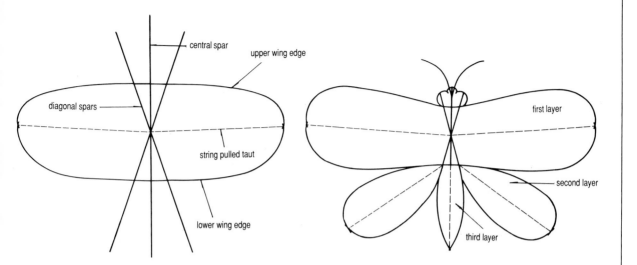

30. **Asterisk-frame.**

32. **Three-layered rigid-wing Bee frame .**

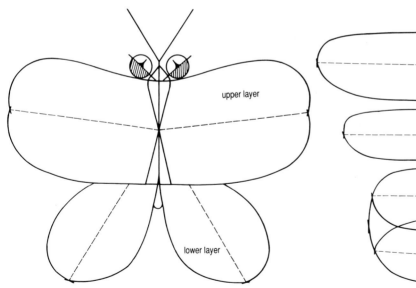

31. **Double-layered rigid-wing Butterfly frame.**

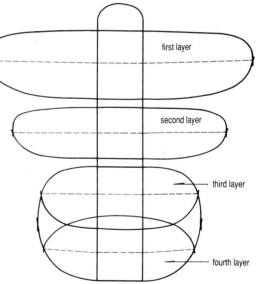

33. **Multi-layered rigid-wing Chinese Character kite frame.**

2. Flexible-wing. The upper wing is defined with bamboo while the lower wing edge is left undefined (fig.34). The frames include single, double and multi-layered types, and designs range from birds to insects and other objects (figs. 35–38; plates 26–30; 32–33). The varieties of designs are frequently very lively, especially when seen in the air.

3. Rigid square-frame. No string is used to bow the frame. Most kites of this type include long tails or tassels. A variety of designs can be applied to this frame including the Eight-trigram, Fish or other objects (figs. 39–40; plates 35–39).

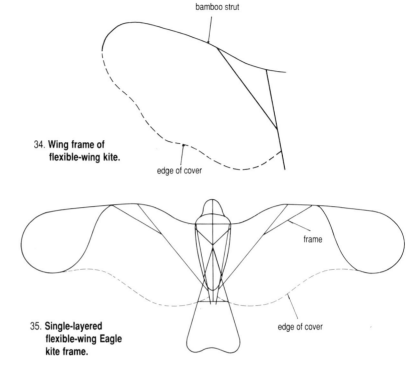

34. **Wing frame of flexible-wing kite.**

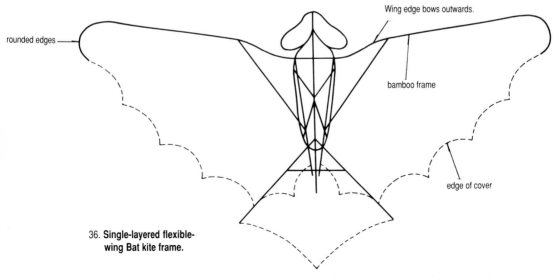

35. **Single-layered flexible-wing Eagle kite frame.**

36. **Single-layered flexible-wing Bat kite frame.**

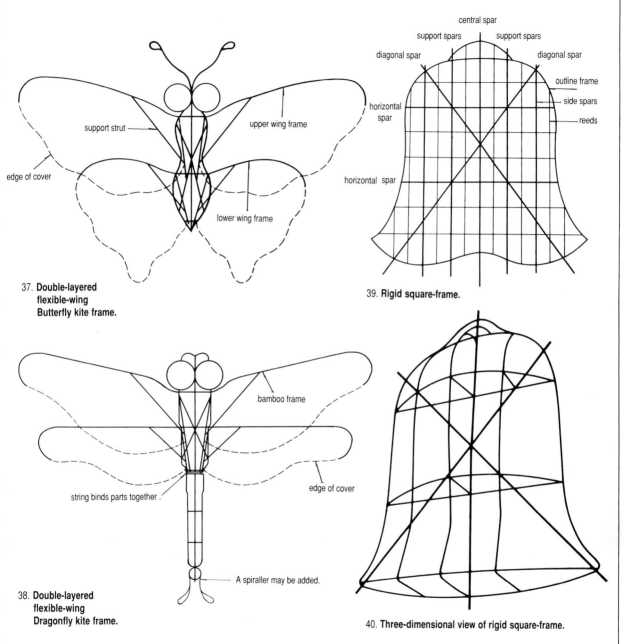

support strut

upper wing frame

edge of cover

lower wing frame

37. **Double-layered
flexible-wing
Butterfly kite frame.**

central spar

support spars   support spars

diagonal spar   diagonal spar

outline frame

side spars

horizontal
spar   reeds

horizontal spar

39. **Rigid square-frame.**

bamboo frame

string binds parts together.

edge of cover

A spiraller may be added.

38. **Double-layered
flexible-wing
Dragonfly kite frame.**

40. **Three-dimensional view of rigid square-frame.**

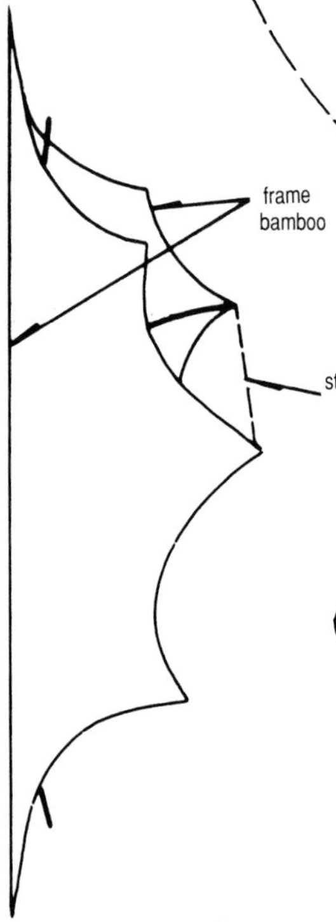

string pulled taut

bamboo

frame bamboo

string pulled taut

41. Flexible square-frame Eight Trigrams kite.

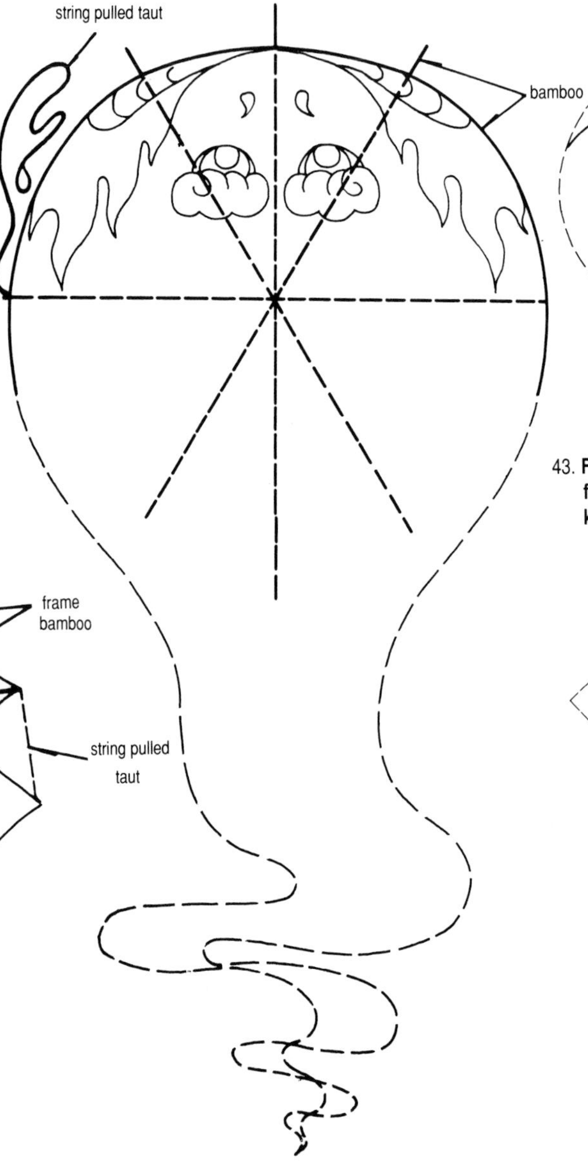

42. Flexible square-frame Tadpole kite. frame.

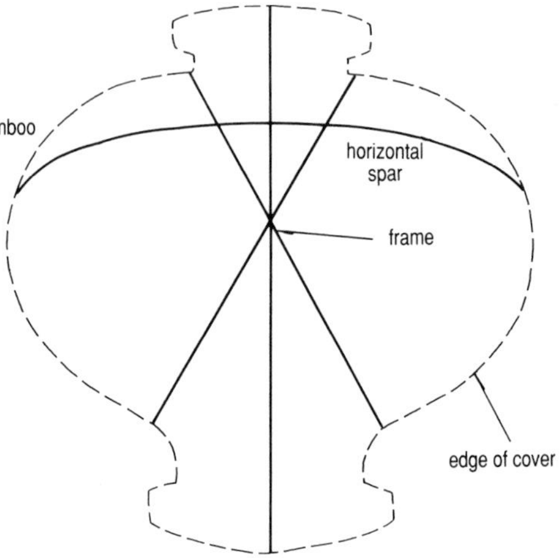

horizontal spar

frame

edge of cover

43. Flexible square-frame Pot-Shaped kite frame.

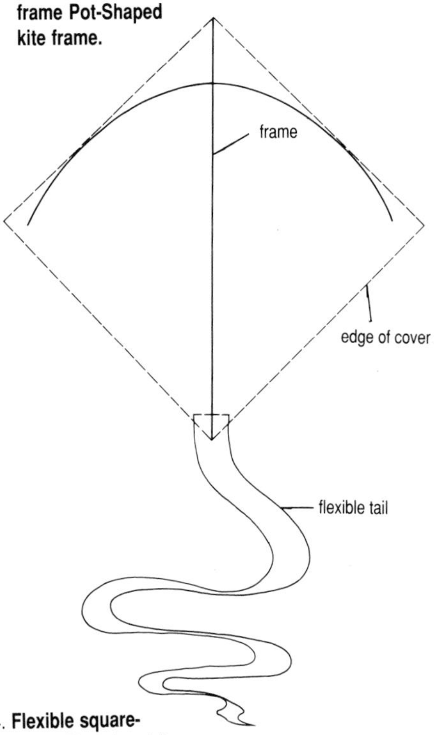

frame

edge of cover

flexible tail

44. Flexible square-frame Rhombus kite.

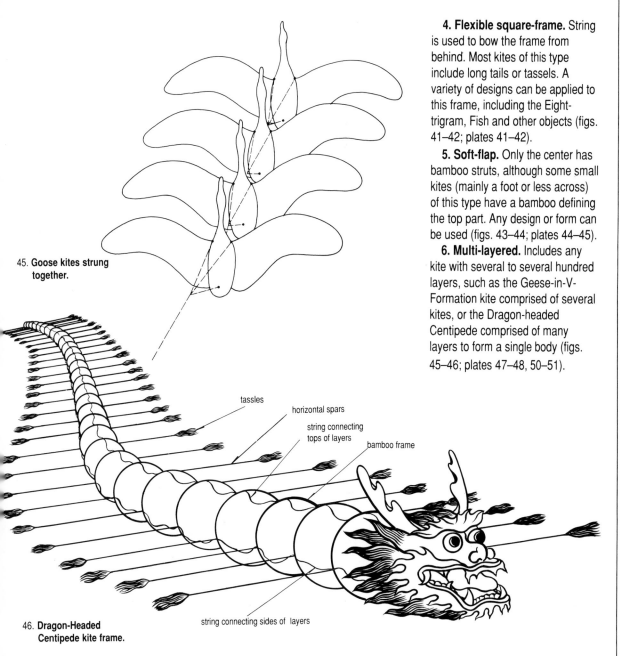

4. Flexible square-frame. String is used to bow the frame from behind. Most kites of this type include long tails or tassels. A variety of designs can be applied to this frame, including the Eight-trigram, Fish and other objects (figs. 41–42; plates 41–42).

5. Soft-flap. Only the center has bamboo struts, although some small kites (mainly a foot or less across) of this type have a bamboo defining the top part. Any design or form can be used (figs. 43–44; plates 44–45).

6. Multi-layered. Includes any kite with several to several hundred layers, such as the Geese-in-V-Formation kite comprised of several kites, or the Dragon-headed Centipede comprised of many layers to form a single body (figs. 45–46; plates 47–48, 50–51).

45. **Goose kites strung together.**

tassles

horizontal spars

string connecting tops of layers

bamboo frame

string connecting sides of layers

46. **Dragon-Headed Centipede kite frame.**

7. Umbrella-type. This type of kite has a triangular framework for support. It also has various frameless, radial shapes, or a combination of these with the triangular. The subject of the kite may be freely chosen by the designer (figs. 47–49; plates 52–55).

8. Three-dimensional. This type of kite includes those with either abstract or concrete three-dimensional shapes. It may have any theme the designer chooses (figs. 50–51; plates 57–58).

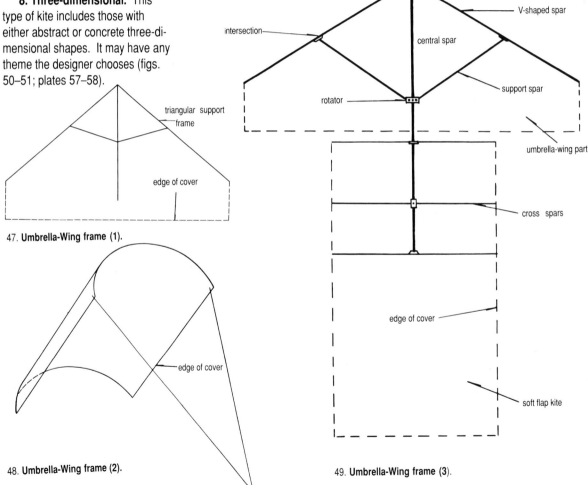

47. **Umbrella-Wing frame (1).**

48. **Umbrella-Wing frame (2).**

49. **Umbrella-Wing frame (3).**

32

50. **Double Rhombus three-dimensional kite frame.**

33

51. **Double Bucket three-dimensional kite frame.**

52. **Gong and Drum.**

53. **Hummer.**

54. **Whistles.**

55. **Blinking Eye.**

56. **Spiraller.**

Apart from the major frame works, the eight basic types of kites discussed here can have various accessories attached to their frames. These accessories do not fly by themselves, but they can add action and sound, using the "special effects" of gongs, drums, organs, whistles, blinking eyes, spirals and a "feeder," or "hurrier" which races up and down the towline (figs. 52–57 on facing page).

57. **Food-Sender or Hurrier.**

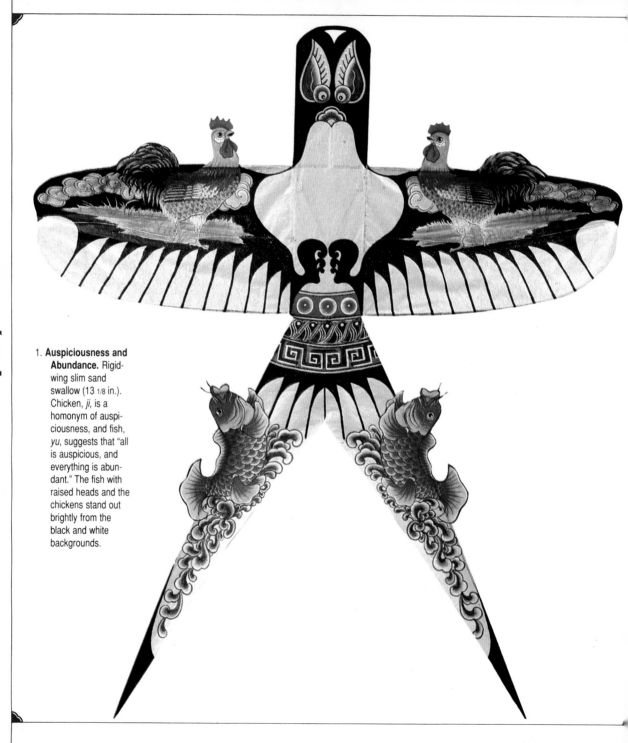

1. **Auspiciousness and Abundance.** Rigid-wing slim sand swallow (13 1/8 in.). Chicken, *ji,* is a homonym of auspiciousness, and fish, *yu,* suggests that "all is auspicious, and everything is abundant." The fish with raised heads and the chickens stand out brightly from the black and white backgrounds.

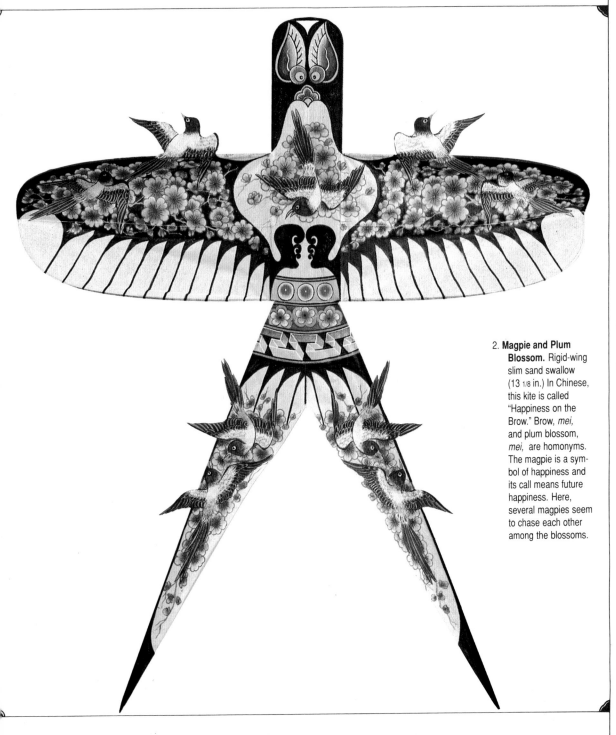

2. **Magpie and Plum Blossom.** Rigid-wing slim sand swallow (13 1/8 in.) In Chinese, this kite is called "Happiness on the Brow." Brow, *mei,* and plum blossom, *mei,* are homonyms. The magpie is a symbol of happiness and its call means future happiness. Here, several magpies seem to chase each other among the blossoms.

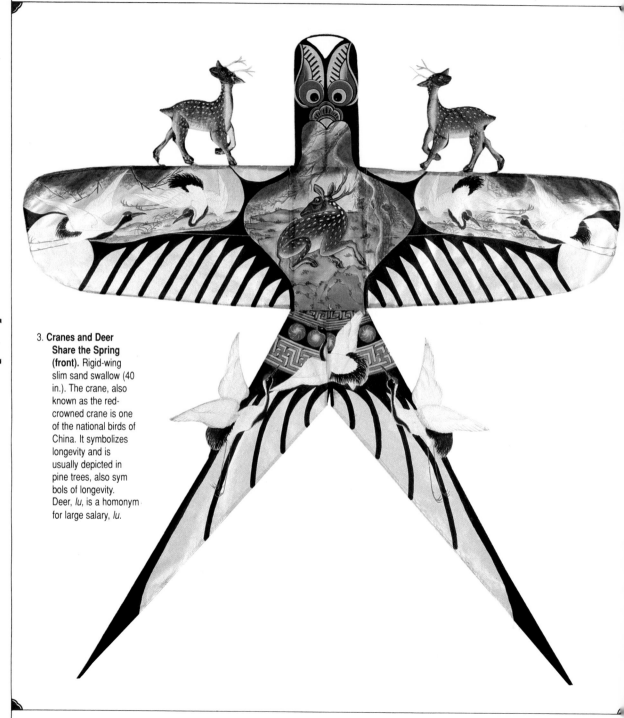

3. **Cranes and Deer Share the Spring (front).** Rigid-wing slim sand swallow (40 in.). The crane, also known as the red-crowned crane is one of the national birds of China. It symbolizes longevity and is usually depicted in pine trees, also sym bols of longevity. Deer, *lu*, is a homonym for large salary, *lu*.

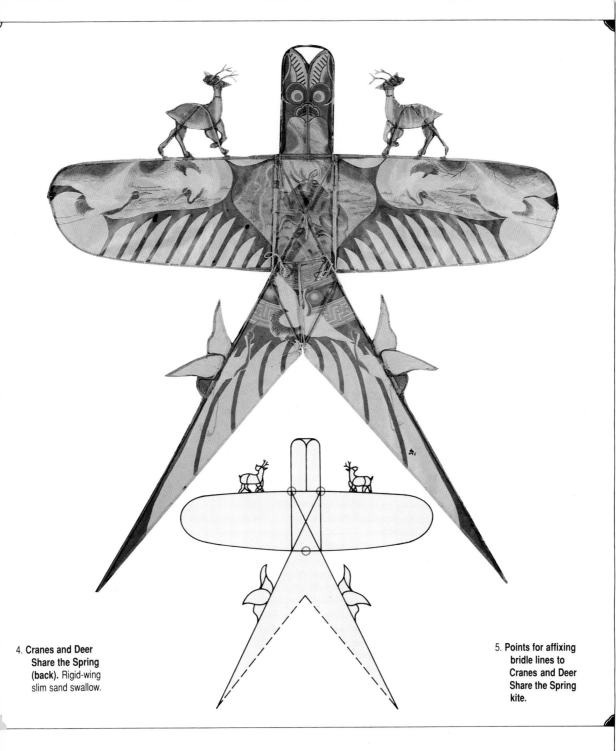

4. **Cranes and Deer Share the Spring (back).** Rigid-wing slim sand swallow.

5. **Points for affixing bridle lines to Cranes and Deer Share the Spring kite.**

6. **Two Dragons Play With a Pearl.** Rigid-wing wide sand swallow (40 in.). The dragon is a god and symbolizes good fortune. Here, a male and a female dragon sport with a pearl. The pearl comes from the male dragon's stomach and when spat out is followed by flames.

7. **Thirteen Bats.** Rigid-wing wide sand swallow (40 in.). This traditional design has a stylized black and white background. The thirteen bats are a symbol of honesty and integrity. The design is popular during the Chinese New Year.

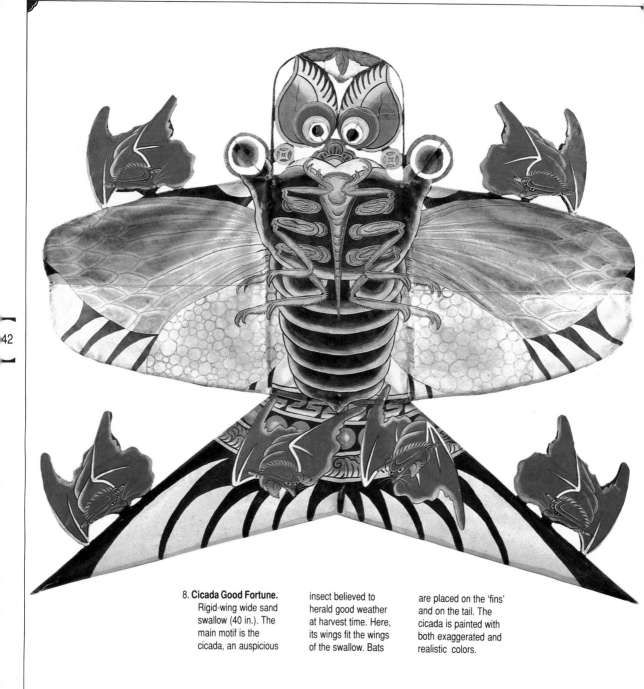

8. **Cicada Good Fortune.**
Rigid-wing wide sand swallow (40 in.). The main motif is the cicada, an auspicious insect believed to herald good weather at harvest time. Here, its wings fit the wings of the swallow. Bats are placed on the 'fins' and on the tail. The cicada is painted with both exaggerated and realistic colors.

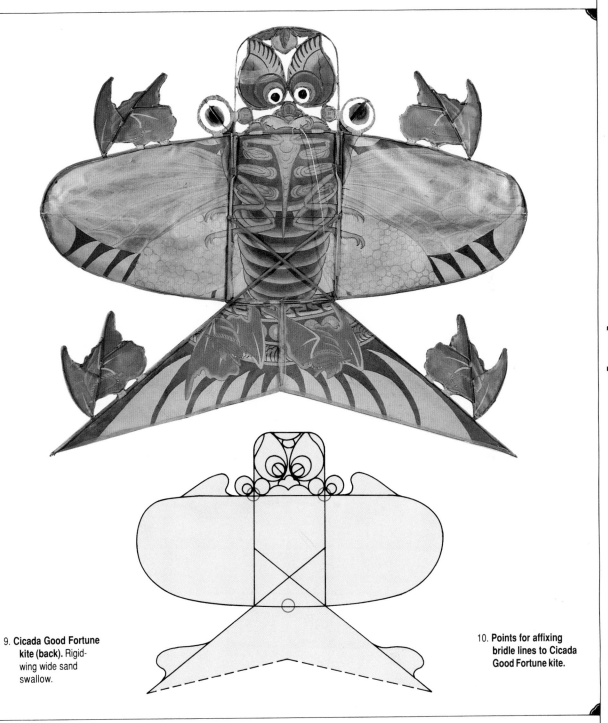

9. **Cicada Good Fortune kite (back).** Rigid-wing wide sand swallow.

10. **Points for affixing bridle lines to Cicada Good Fortune kite.**

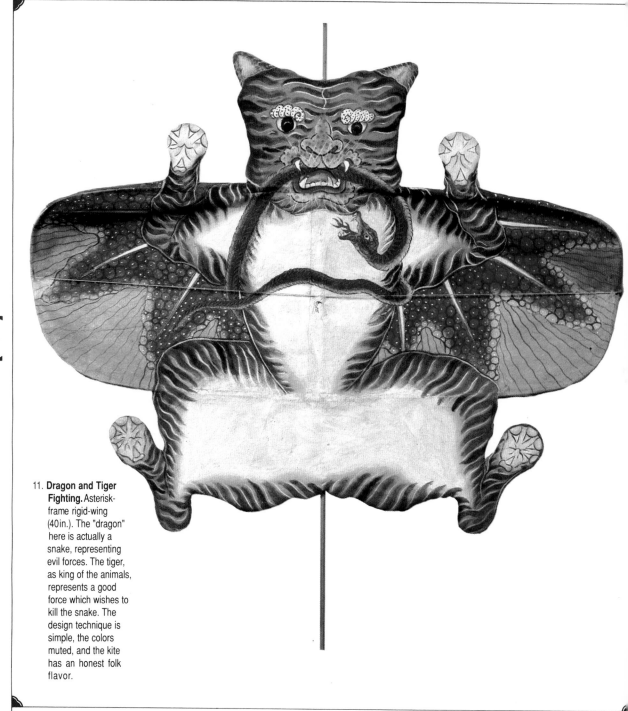

11. **Dragon and Tiger Fighting.** Asterisk-frame rigid-wing (40 in.). The "dragon" here is actually a snake, representing evil forces. The tiger, as king of the animals, represents a good force which wishes to kill the snake. The design technique is simple, the colors muted, and the kite has an honest folk flavor.

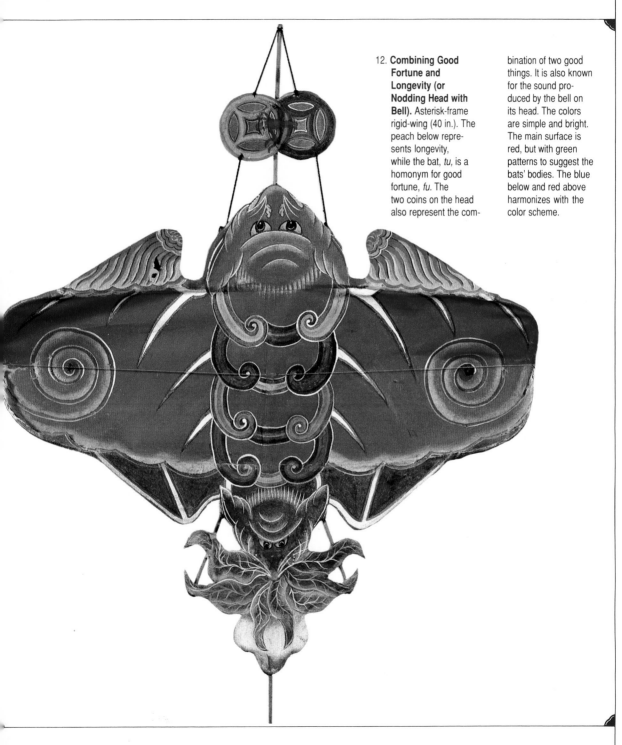

12. **Combining Good Fortune and Longevity (or Nodding Head with Bell).** Asterisk-frame rigid-wing (40 in.). The peach below represents longevity, while the bat, *tu,* is a homonym for good fortune, *fu.* The two coins on the head also represent the combination of two good things. It is also known for the sound produced by the bell on its head. The colors are simple and bright. The main surface is red, but with green patterns to suggest the bats' bodies. The blue below and red above harmonizes with the color scheme.

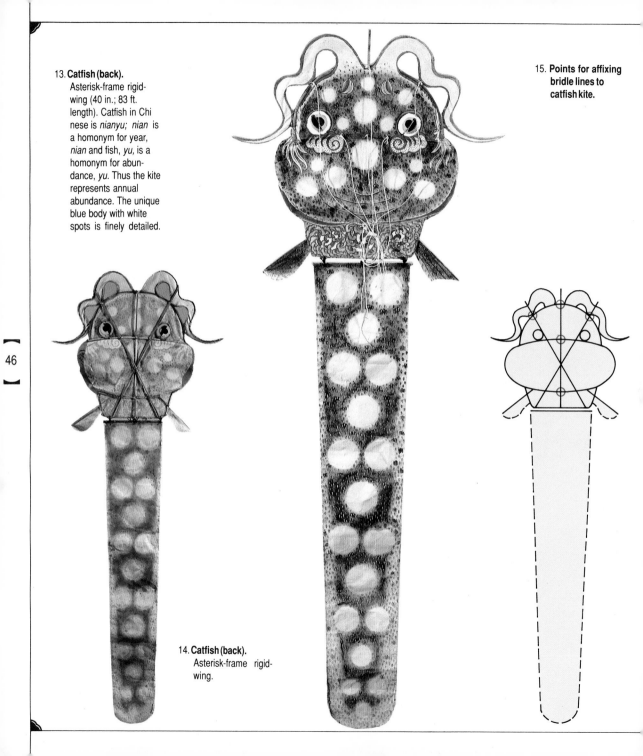

13. **Catfish (back).**
    Asterisk-frame rigid-
    wing (40 in.; 83 ft.
    length). Catfish in Chi
    nese is *nianyu; nian* is
    a homonym for year,
    nian and fish, *yu,* is a
    homonym for abun-
    dance, *yu.* Thus the kite
    represents annual
    abundance. The unique
    blue body with white
    spots is finely detailed.

15. **Points for affixing
    bridle lines to
    catfish kite.**

14. **Catfish (back).**
    Asterisk-frame rigid-
    wing.

16. **Two Immortals.**
Asterisk-frame rigid-wing (53 in.). A boy and a girl traditionally represent a happy life among friends, between man and wife, or general accord among people. The box, *he,* in the girl's hand and the lotus leaf, *he,* in the boy's, represent accord, *hehe.* Their smiles are the epitome of happiness.

17. **Nezha Stirs Up the Sea (front).** Asterisk-frame rigid wing (40 in.) The story is from the Ming dynasty novel, *Fenshen yanyi,* in which Nezha is a Buddhist god able to change his form, stand on wheels of fire, and hold a sacred halberd and ring. Folk origins are apparent in the bright colors and brisk style. The five wheels actually move as if Nezha is flying.

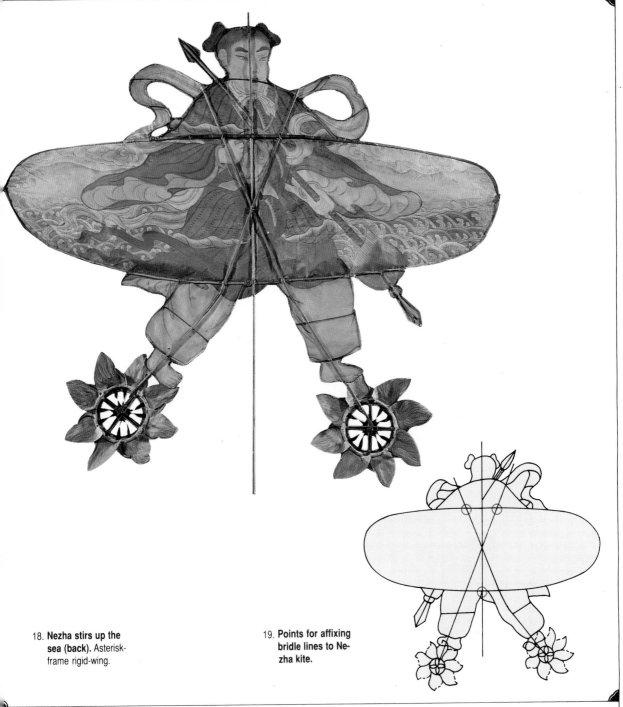

18. **Nezha stirs up the sea (back).** Asterisk-frame rigid-wing.

19. **Points for affixing bridle lines to Ne-zha kite.**

20. **Peony Butterfly.**
Asterisk-frame rigid-
wing (5 1/4 in.). A

basic asterisk frame
with an exaggerated
butterfly decoration.

Radiating layers of
purple suggest the
petals of the peony.

21. **Red Dragonfly.**
Double-layered rigid-wing (7 7/8 in.). The two wings of this kite are based on the single-layered rigid-wing kite frame. The even-lined, forward-bowing upper wing edge of the rigid-wing kite becomes the more rising and curving wing. The lower wing remains shorter, adding to the realism of the design.

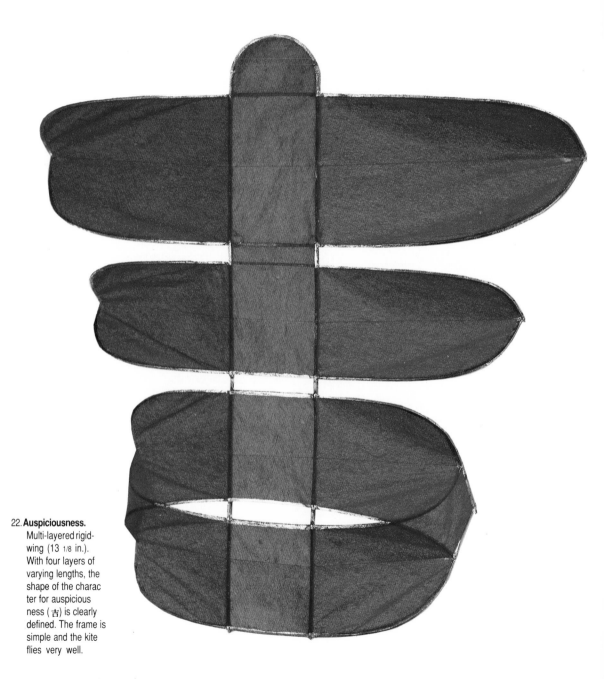

52

22. **Auspiciousness.**
Multi-layered rigid-
wing (13 1/8 in.).
With four layers of
varying lengths, the
shape of the charac
ter for auspicious
ness (吉) is clearly
defined. The frame is
simple and the kite
flies very well.

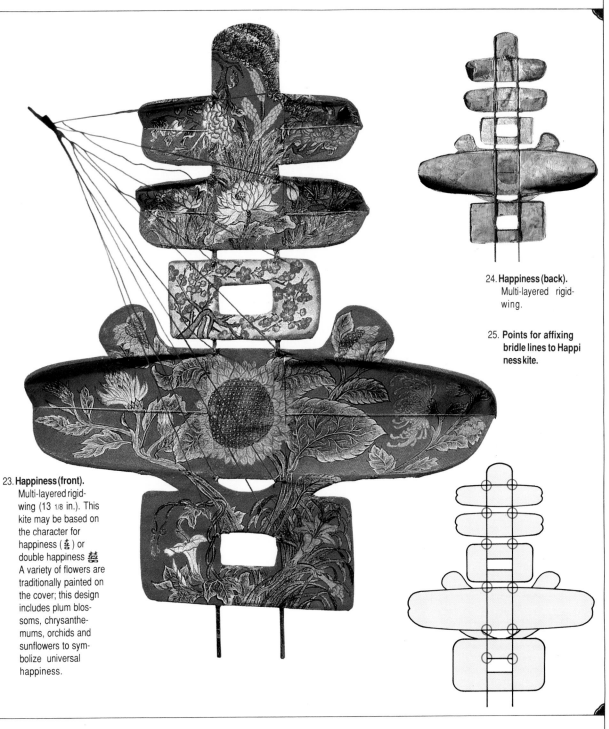

23. Happiness (front).
Multi-layered rigid-
wing (13 1/8 in.). This
kite may be based on
the character for
happiness (壴) or
double happiness 囍
A variety of flowers are
traditionally painted on
the cover; this design
includes plum blos-
soms, chrysanthe-
mums, orchids and
sunflowers to sym-
bolize universal
happiness.

24. Happiness (back).
Multi-layered rigid-
wing.

**25. Points for affixing
bridle lines to Happi
ness kite.**

26. **Heron.** Single-layered flexible-wing (40 in.). The design is based on the heron and is painted using traditional Chinese techniques of fine brushwork and detail. First the outline is drawn and then the colors are applied in layers of washes.

27. **Red Dragonfly.**
Double-layered flexi-
ble-wing (40 in.). This
kite achieves a real-
istic yet decorative
effect. The shoulders
rise above the head to
increase the wind
resistance area. The
eyes and tail can ro-
tate. The colors are
rich yet translucent
and have a certain
folk flavor.

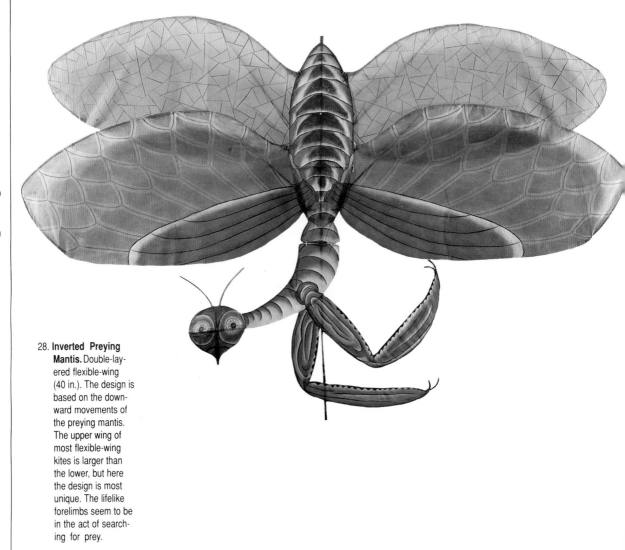

28. **Inverted Preying Mantis.** Double-layered flexible-wing (40 in.). The design is based on the downward movements of the preying mantis. The upper wing of most flexible-wing kites is larger than the lower, but here the design is most unique. The lifelike forelimbs seem to be in the act of searching for prey.

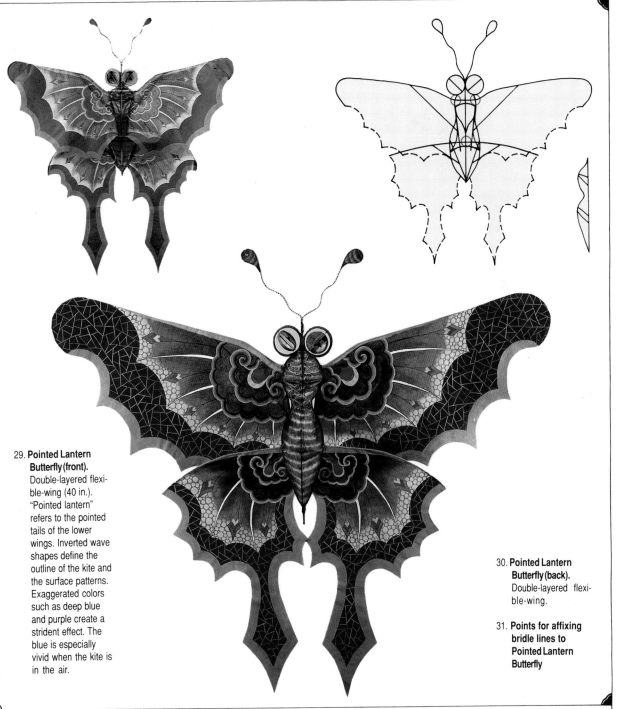

29. **Pointed Lantern Butterfly (front).** Double-layered flexi-ble-wing (40 in.). "Pointed lantern" refers to the pointed tails of the lower wings. Inverted wave shapes define the outline of the kite and the surface patterns. Exaggerated colors such as deep blue and purple create a strident effect. The blue is especially vivid when the kite is in the air.

30. **Pointed Lantern Butterfly (back).** Double-layered flexi-ble-wing.

31. **Points for affixing bridle lines to Pointed Lantern Butterfly**

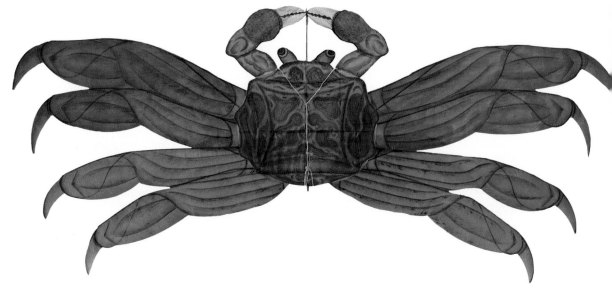

32. **Crab (front).** Multi-layered flexible-wing (40 in.). The frame is composed of four flexible wings and is extremely realistic. Light and dark green and black are used and fine brush strokes define the spirals on the crab's back, though the design is generally unfussy.

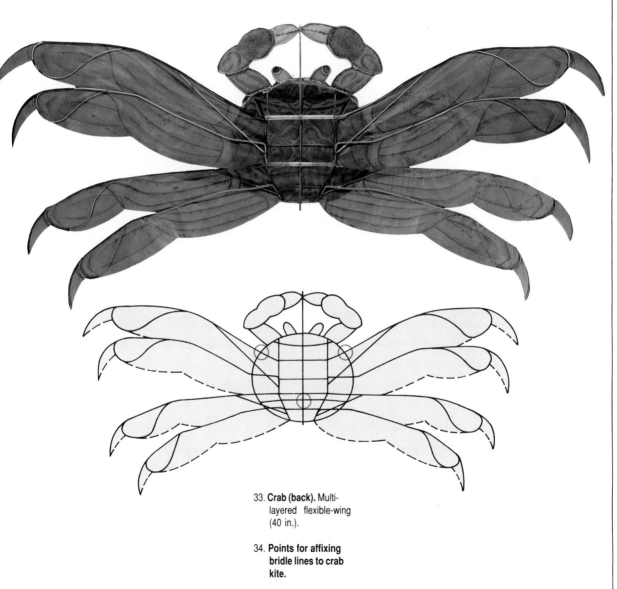

59

33. **Crab (back).** Multi-layered flexible-wing (40 in.).

34. **Points for affixing bridle lines to crab kite.**

35. **Bronze Incense Burner.** Rigid square-frame (40 in.). The design is based on temple incense burners. Fierce lions guard the water. The colors lend an air of antiquity to the design.

60

36. **Flower Vase.** Rigid square-frame (40 in.). The artwork is based on a traditional Chinese vase depicting "Goddess Guanyin Sending Sons." Guanyin (Avalokitesvara) is one of the principal bodhisattvas who remain on earth to help mankind. Here, Guanyin sends sons to families lacking male heirs.

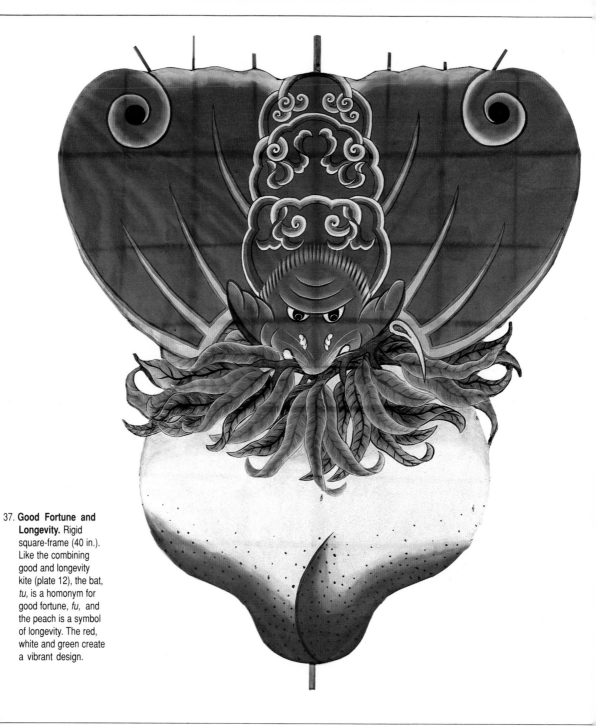

37. **Good Fortune and Longevity.** Rigid square-frame (40 in.). Like the combining good and longevity kite (plate 12), the bat, *tu,* is a homonym for good fortune, *fu,* and the peach is a symbol of longevity. The red, white and green create a vibrant design.

38. **Frog (front).** Rigid square-frame (40 in.). Also called "Gold Thread Frog." Because the frog consumes so many insect pests, it is often considered a protecting god. It was also believed to devour monsters. The design is close to its folk art source with relatively simple colors.

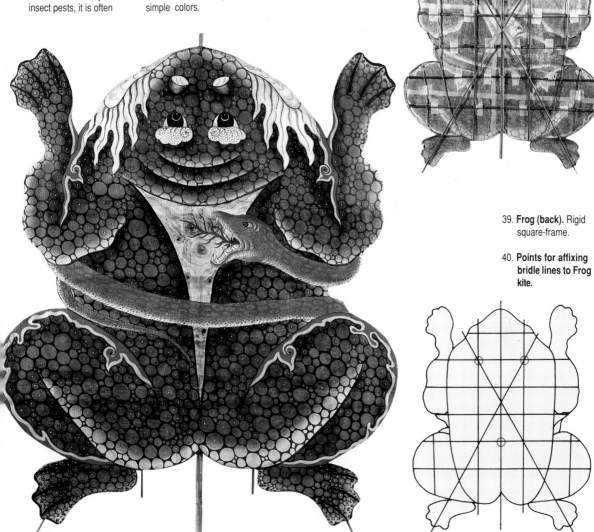

39. **Frog (back).** Rigid square-frame.

40. **Points for affixing bridle lines to Frog kite.**

41. **Eight Trigrams.**
    Flexible square-frame
    (40 in.). The eight tri-
    grams were devised in
    ancient China as a set
    of oracle-like figures,
    traditionally supposed
    to have been invented
    by Fu Xishi. They are
    also used for geo-
    mancy and divination.

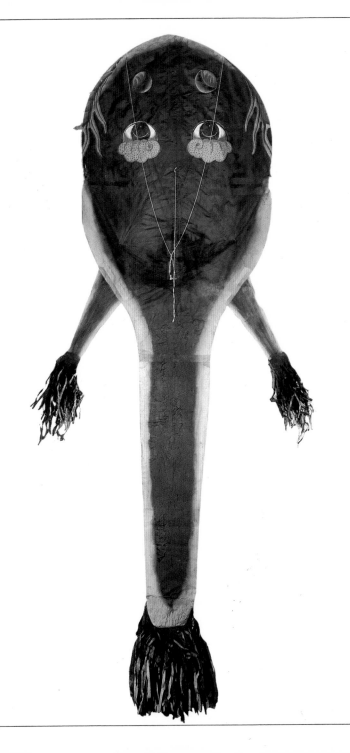

42. **Tadpole.** Flexible square-frame (40 in.). The design is comparatively realistic in shape and color although the facial features are exaggerated for decorative purposes.

43. **Points for attaching bridle lines to Tadpole kite.**

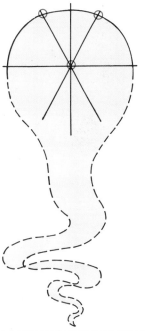

44. **Pot-Shaped kite.**
Soft-flap (13 1/8 in.).
The design is rela-
tively simple, the col-
ors are bright and ap-
plied without detail.
Because of its size
and simplicity, the
cover edges are un
supported and it is
only flown in light
winds. Many
children in China fly
this type of kite.

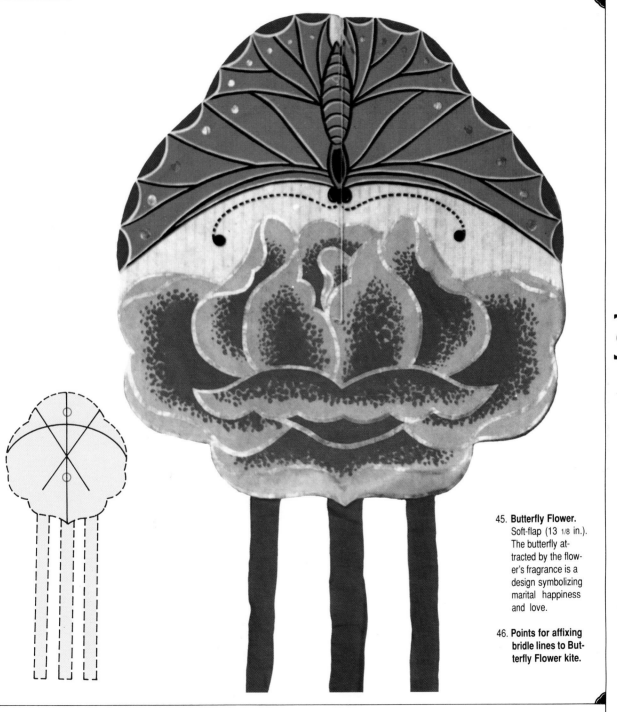

45. **Butterfly Flower.**
Soft-flap (13 1/8 in.).
The butterfly at-
tracted by the flow-
er's fragrance is a
design symbolizing
marital happiness
and love.

46. **Points for affixing
bridle lines to But-
terfly Flower kite.**

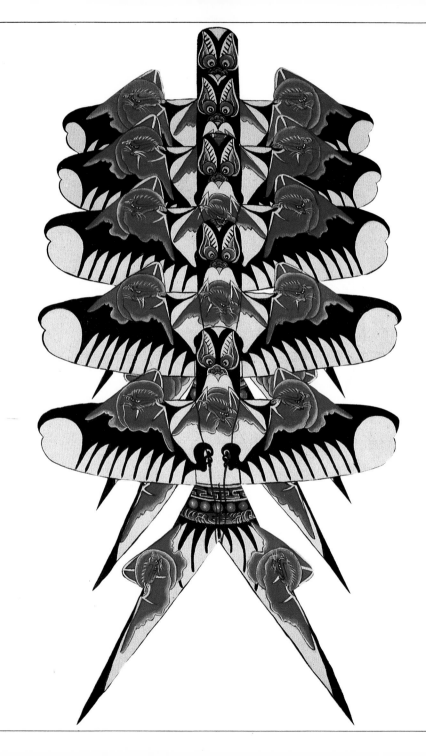

47. **Layered Sand Swallows.** Multi-layered (40 in.; 24 ft. length). Seven slim sand swallow kites are strung together to create a particularly lovely flight effect. Generally flown in strong winds because it is multi-layered.

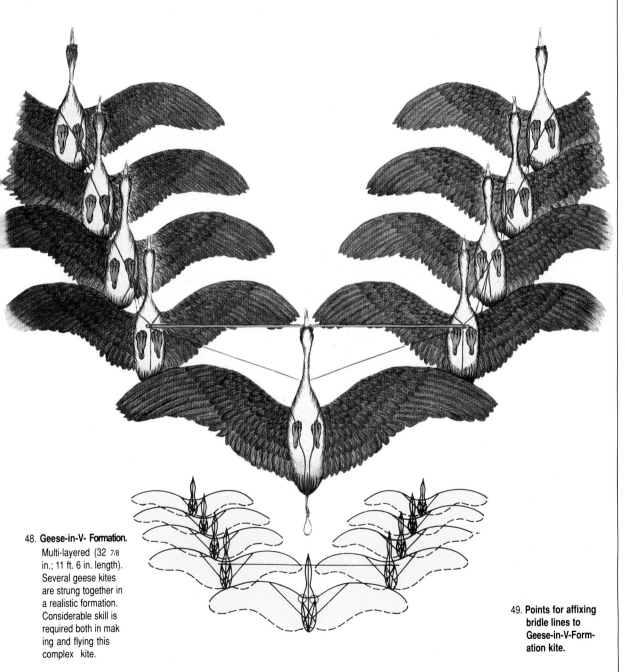

48. **Geese-in-V- Formation.**
Multi-layered (32 7/8
in.; 11 ft. 6 in. length).
Several geese kites
are strung together in
a realistic formation.
Considerable skill is
required both in mak
ing and flying this
complex kite.

49. **Points for affixing
bridle lines to
Geese-in-V-Form-
ation kite.**

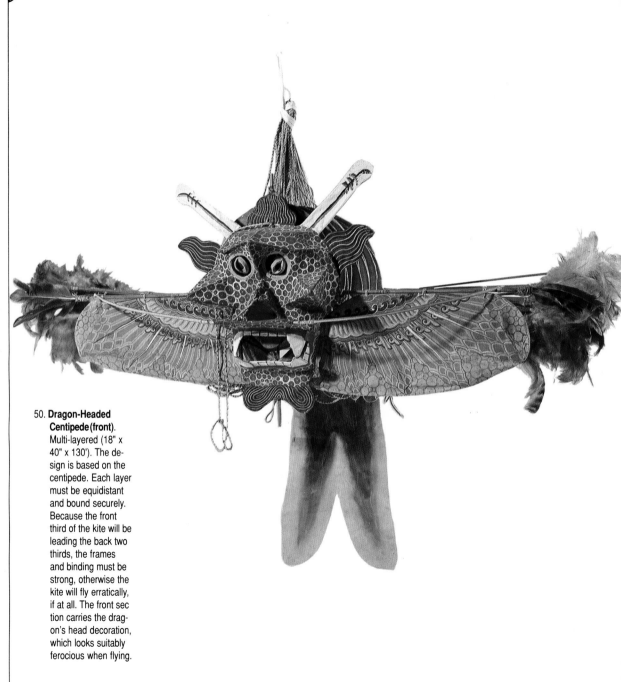

50. **Dragon-Headed Centipede (front)**. Multi-layered (18" x 40" x 130'). The design is based on the centipede. Each layer must be equidistant and bound securely. Because the front third of the kite will be leading the back two thirds, the frames and binding must be strong, otherwise the kite will fly erratically, if at all. The front sec tion carries the drag on's head decoration, which looks suitably ferocious when flying.

51. **Dragon-Headed
    Centipede (back).**
    Multi-layered.

52. **Red Phoenix and
Rising Sun.** Um-
brella-wing. (40
in.).Legend says the
phoenix was born in
the red cave of the
South, from which the
sun rises. The morning
sun symbolizes good
luck. The phoenix will
only alight in Chinese
parasol trees and eat
certain bamboos. The
design includes
peonies which,
together with the
phoenix, stand for
marital harmony and
love. The painting
technique here is
traditional Chinese
brush style.

53. **The Goddess of the Luo River.** Umbrella-wing (40 in.). Known as Miifei, the goddess of this river is traditionally supposed to be the daughter of Fu Xishi. After drowning herself in the Luo River, she becomes a river goddess. Cao Zhi describes her exceptional beauty in his poem, "The Goddess of the Luo River."

54. **Heavenly Judge (front).** Umbrella-wing (40 in.). Zhong Kui is the mythical figure who failed one exam in the rigorous imperial examinations. In a fit of mortification, he dashed himself to death from some steps. In the afterworld he vowed to eradicate all the evils in the empire and was made a god by the Jade Emperor.

55. **Heavenly Judge (back). Umbrella-wing.**

56. **Points for affixing bridle lines to Heavenly Judge kite.**

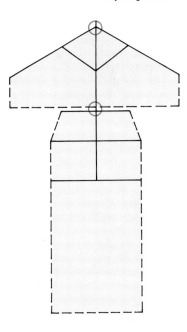

57. **Door Lantern.** Three-dimensional (26 1/4 in.) This simple and realistic design is based on a traditional Chinese lantern. It only requires a one-leg bridle.

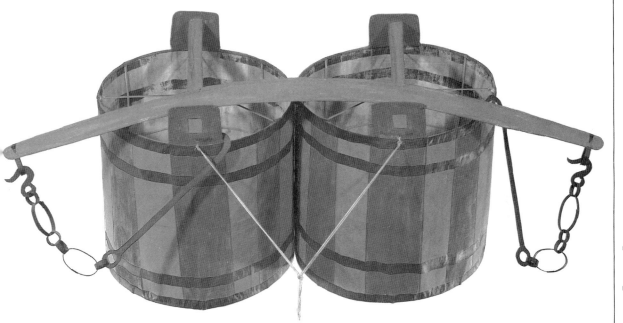

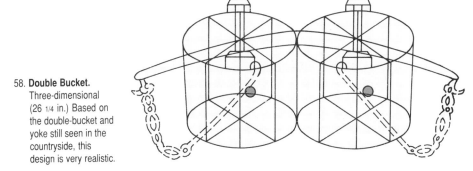

58. **Double Bucket.**
    Three-dimensional
    (26 1/4 in.) Based on
    the double-bucket and
    yoke still seen in the
    countryside, this
    design is very realistic.

59. **Points for affixing
    bridle lines to
    Double-Bucket kite.**

Chapter
3
Construction
and
Art
of
Ha
Family
Kites

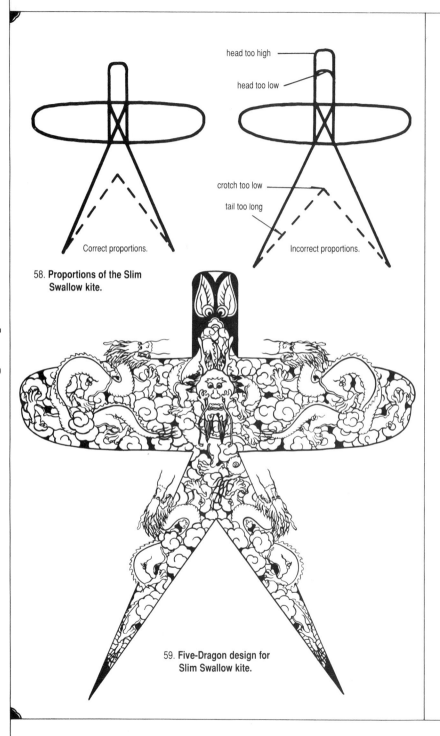

head too high

head too low

crotch too low

tail too long

Correct proportions.

Incorrect proportions.

58. **Proportions of the Slim Swallow kite.**

59. **Five-Dragon design for Slim Swallow kite.**

The Ha kite-makers have not only continued their own traditions, but have also incorporated techniques of other kitemakers. By creating new kite forms and by experimenting with structural patterns and decorative designs, they have integrated technique with art in their characteristic style. Below are some concrete examples of modifications and new forms.

Frame construction. The dimensions of each part of the kite should be proportional and join exactly, while the structural and decorative elements should be harmonious to insure an overall pleasing appearance. It is necessary to consider the strength required of the supports so that they will be evenly spaced and achieve a balance between light weight and durability.

Each part of the framework must be carefully measured in proportion to the body. Consider the Sand Swallow kite composed of two wings which are functional parts, and a tail, a head and four "fins" which are decorative parts. These should all be proportionate to the size of the kite. The decorative design must correspond too, otherwise the overall effect of the kite in the air will not be so dramatic. Decorations are based on actual works of art and principles of proportion. For example, the head of a figure must not be placed too high or low because this would make the neck appear either too elongated or compressed. Similarly, if tails are too long they take on a stilt-like appearance, yet they must not be excessively short (fig. 58). The neat joints and overall pleasing appearance mentioned above are achieved by integrating construction with aesthetics. The basic frame is constructed first, then the decorative parts added.

The organization of the chosen design must then be considered. The Five Dragon Swallow is a good example (fig. 59; plate 62). The design is composed of five dragons, four of which are placed respectively on each "limb" with their heads protruding. It is important to consider how far the heads project because too much protrusion impairs the flying performance. However, too little protrusion harms the design. Painting all five dragons on the two wings would make the design cluttered and unattractive. Good craftsmanship is essential to insure that the heads and bodies of the dragons are fixed in their corresponding positions. Once a pleasant arrangement of the five dragons is achieved to harmonize the body of the kite, then construction and aesthetics are integrated.

The rigid-wing Sand Swallow kite is based on the actual shape of a swallow in flight, although the design is slightly exaggerated. This particular kite form is one of the most representative in China; its

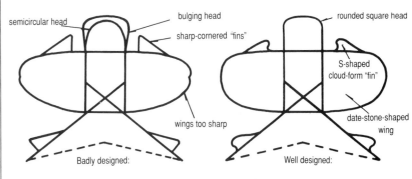

60. **Comparison of Wide Swallow frames.**

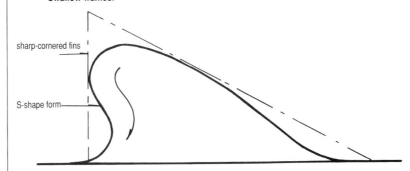

61. **S-shaped cloud form "fin."**
The "fin" is defined as a curve and is called cloud form because it resembles clouds in Chinese paintings.

62. **S-shaped cloud-form "fin."**

81

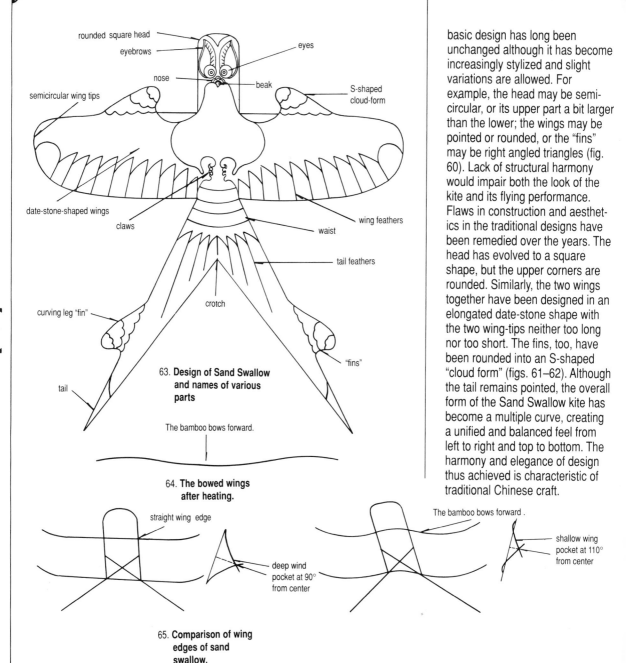

rounded square head

eyebrows

eyes

nose

beak

S-shaped cloud-form

semicircular wing tips

date-stone-shaped wings

claws

wing feathers

waist

tail feathers

curving leg "fin"

crotch

"fins"

tail

63. **Design of Sand Swallow and names of various parts**

The bamboo bows forward.

64. **The bowed wings after heating.**

straight wing edge

deep wind pocket at 90° from center

The bamboo bows forward .

shallow wing pocket at 110° from center

65. **Comparison of wing edges of sand swallow.**

basic design has long been unchanged although it has become increasingly stylized and slight variations are allowed. For example, the head may be semi-circular, or its upper part a bit larger than the lower; the wings may be pointed or rounded, or the "fins" may be right angled triangles (fig. 60). Lack of structural harmony would impair both the look of the kite and its flying performance. Flaws in construction and aesthet-ics in the traditional designs have been remedied over the years. The head has evolved to a square shape, but the upper corners are rounded. Similarly, the two wings together have been designed in an elongated date-stone shape with the two wing-tips neither too long nor too short. The fins, too, have been rounded into an S-shaped "cloud form" (figs. 61–62). Although the tail remains pointed, the overall form of the Sand Swallow kite has become a multiple curve, creating a unified and balanced feel from left to right and top to bottom. The harmony and elegance of design thus achieved is characteristic of traditional Chinese craft.

Strengthening the frame materials and the binding for greater wind-resistance.

Example 1. The upper and lower edges of the wings of traditional or common rigid-wing kites are flat and create a straight, smooth surface. The wing tips are usually curved at 90° to form a deep wind pocket. The Ha family uses this basic method, but instead of leaving the upper and lower edges of the wings straight, they are bowed by heating to curve forward (fig. 64). This means that the wing tips will curve at an angle of 110° to form a shallow wind pocket (fig. 65). With the wings bowed forward, the kite becomes more resilient and elastic, air currents lift it easily and its wind resistance is 30% greater than kites without this modification. The strong bowed wings appear like the arms of a weight lifter.

Example 2. Traditionally, the upper edge of the flexible-wing kite is only slightly bowed outwards and upwards and the tips of the wings are not curved. This reduces the kite's wind resistance and lifting power. The Has have increased the wind resistance and enriched the design of flexible-wing kites, especially the butterfly, dragonfly and frog types, by bowing the upper part of the wing more prominently upwards and forwards and by rounding the wing-tips. If the wind is strong, this form of flexible-wing kite will keep its stability and angle of attack (fig. 66).

Example 3. The rigid square-frame type kite has also had its basic structure improved and modified for greater strength. Although resembling early twentieth-century kites in construction, the materials used for the modern kite have greater wind resistance. The traditional kite used bamboo struts only .2" in diameter as central and cross spars and was comparatively fragile. Simply using struts of .4" or more doubles the strength, making this prototype one of China's strongest in this class of wind resistance (fig. 39).

Example 4. To increase the strength of the upper and lower wing edges on comparatively large rigid-wing kites, a separate bamboo strut is glued to the inside of each wing strip (fig.106).

Achieving a perfect combination of artistry and technique by improving the traditional frame composition.

Example 1. The traditional three-layered rigid-wing Frog kite is made up of three wing layers which cause the kite to hop and flap in the air (fig. 67). The first layer consists of the forelegs and the shoulders, the second consists of the stomach and the third of the rear legs and hind quarters. The Has widened the second layer to make the proportions of the body more naturalistic and also improved the design of the head, mouth and feet for a more convincing effect. The widening of the second layer also increases wind resistance and flying perform-

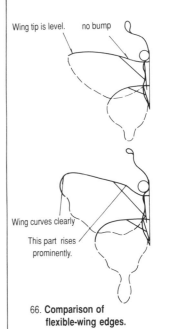

Wing tip is level.   no bump

Wing curves clearly

This part rises prominently.

66. **Comparison of flexible-wing edges.**

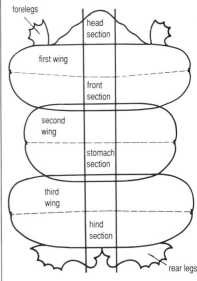

forelegs

head section

first wing

front section

second wing

stomach section

third wing

hind section

rear legs

67. **Multi-layered rigid-wing Frog kite.**

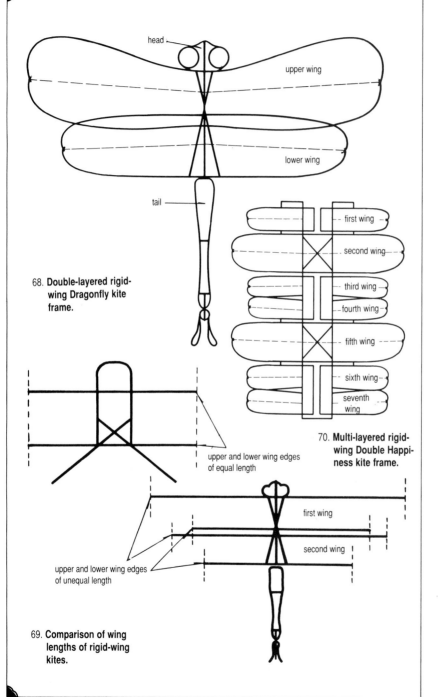

head

upper wing

lower wing

tail

68. **Double-layered rigid-wing Dragonfly kite frame.**

- first wing
- second wing
- third wing
- fourth wing
- fifth wing
- sixth wing
- seventh wing

70. **Multi-layered rigid-wing Double Happiness kite frame.**

upper and lower wing edges of equal length

first wing

second wing

upper and lower wing edges of unequal length

69. **Comparison of wing lengths of rigid-wing kites.**

ance, especially in strong winds.

Example 2. The rigid-wing Dragonfly kite has two main wings and two lesser wings (fig. 68). The top edges of the wings are longer than the bottom edges and curve upwards and outwards. The main wings are longer than the lesser wings. One of the modifications in the original design was to lengthen the main wings and shorten the lesser wings, which were traditionally equal. If the wings are equal, the overall effect is discordant and lacks realism (fig. 69). When the wings have been made, they should be joined to the body along with the head and tail. The revised design of this kite is based on both the flexible-wing kite and the rigid-wing kite for greater wind resistance.

Example 3. The rigid-wing Double Happiness kite is composed of seven rigid wings (fig. 70). Because of the peculiarities of the shape of the Chinese character, there are two apertures, one between the third and fourth layers, and one between the sixth and seventh layers respectively. The frame is made up of two vertical spars and two cross-shaped supports. There are no further additions to the design as each of the seven layers is capable of lifting the kite, making flight comparatively easy.

Example 4. Some decorative parts of kites are particularly exquisite and finely crafted, such as the more complicated "fin" designs on the sand swallow kite or the careful outlines on the kites featuring human figures. The outward appearance of these parts varies according to the subject. The inter-joining of the decorative parts to the frame is perfected by careful selection of bamboo struts according to the specifications of the design and decoration, and careful heating and bending and good binding of the joints (figs. 71-74; plates 61 and 74;).

Creating new types and improving kite attachments.

Example 1. The Double-flag kite is a new type of flexible-wing kite (figs. 75-76). The frame is simply composed of two flag shapes bound together, easily achieving a realistic effect.

Example 2. The Umbrella kite is a new type of kite that combines the soft-flap type kite (the bottom part), and the umbrella-wing type kite (the triangular top part) (fig. 49). Construction, design, appearance and flying performance are all improved by this simple combination (plate 91).

Example 3. The "blinking eye" accessory is usually circular and formed from two wind boxes (fig.123). This and the four wind boxes have been improved simply by using two circular pieces that cross in the middle (fig. 77) with the angle sloping upwards, enabling all four sides to catch the wind, making the "eye" blink more rapidly for added realism.

Decoration. The Ha artisans strive for greatest effect and beauty with a variety of methods of decoration, such as fine brushwork and close details of traditional Chinese painting, the rules of purely decorative art, dot and line effects or techniques from printing, New Year pictures and sculpture. Thus, kite decoration can be seen as a comprehensive art form. The selection of a particular method of decoration is closely related to the actual kite design, so that its visual effect in the sky will be harmonious and pleasing. If this does not result, the design is regarded as a failure. Similarly, unity of composition and color in the decoration of a kite must be stressed and consideration given to making it seen as a clear, whole image in the sky. For example, the design of the Red Dragon-and-Fish kite achieves both a contrasting effect against the blue of the sky and a pleasing artistic one.

Although there are many different designs, they are not casually applied; application depends on the characteristics of each particular kite. With this aim in mind, each kite will have its special traits based on three factors: theme, design and color.

In terms of theme, kite-making is a folk handicraft with traditional popular themes that reflect some aspect of everyday life, often something in which people could place their hopes. Particular favorites are themes concerning

the future.

Ha family kites with such themes include those with designs from nature (plates 77 and 83); characters from history and myths (plates 74 and 90); and even those invested with favorable portents or with designs that symbolized good luck (plates 64 and 67). There are also a few with no symbolism, but simply a mixture of geometric designs. These may also be considered as decorative themes (plates 89 and 93).

Obviously, the overall design of the kite body must satisfy the dictates of flight. The rigid-wing Sand Swallow is an example of this. Its flight is chiefly dependent on the two wings, while the other elements can be classed as decoration. When constructing the frame, it is important to remember that the overall surface area of the decorative parts must be smaller than the area of the wing span. If it is larger, the kite will simply not fly. Therefore, the decorative theme is generally confined to the main flying parts and within the two wings. For example, the "Great Prosperity Fills the Sky" Sand Swallow kite (plate 63), takes bats as its major motif with clouds as background. The entire design begins from the center of the wings and extends to left and right and top to bottom, so the center becomes the "kernel" of the design. This notion of the kernel is a basic principle of kite design.

71. Dragon Head "fin" on Nine Dragon Swallow kite.

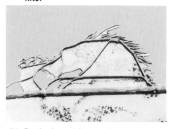

72. Back view of frame of Dragon's Head.

73. Front view of "Zheng Chenggong" decoration.

74. Back view showing frame.

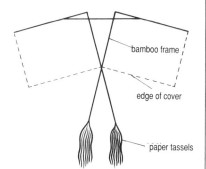

bamboo frame

edge of cover

paper tassels

75. Double-Flag kite frame.

76. Ha Yiqi holds a Double-flag kite featuring flags of China and the U.S. On his left is the chairman of the American Kite Association.

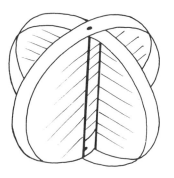

77. The improved "blinking eye" accessory.

The rigid-wing human figure kite with its asterisk-shaped frame has wings basically the same as those of the sand swallow. Because the center of the wings is the major area of wind resistance (it takes up half the surface area of the wings and extends above and below the wing center, though less toward the top), it is the most vital part for successful flying. When the kite is in the air, this part will be the largest and most prominent feature of the design. With the human figure kite this is impossible because a figure or group of figures is normally described from head to foot. To insure effective design, the human figure should take up the whole major flying surface. If the organization of the decoration to the left and right of the frame is unsymmetrical, then a background or some other motif must be added to balance the two sides. The human figure design in itself should be a complete one without further additions, although a cloud-like decoration as background will help to set off the figure clearly (fig. 78; plate 75).

There are major differences among the designs of rigid-wing kites and those of other kites. For example, the designs of flexible-wing kites more frequently employ the forms of certain characters, or animals, birds and insects which, with some changes and additions can achieve a very realistic effect (plates 83 and 86). Regardless of its final form, a completed design should be like a sculpture, with a three dimensional effect—a flying work of art.

Next, the design of the individual parts must be considered. Although there are many different decorative motifs and themes, what is or is not painted is dictated by the central wind-resistance area, which generally has a fixed decorative formula. Some complete designs are formed by incorporating what can be considered as several separate decorative parts. For example, the Five Blessings Proffering Longevity kite (fig. 79), is a complete design with five bats surrounding a large peach, a symbol of longevity. Each bat is a separate part, but combined with the peach, the parts form a harmonious design. Other designs, such as the butterfly, also stress the harmony of the parts and the whole (figs. 80–81).

All kite designs employ two methods: 1) the parts enrich the whole, and 2) the whole sets off the parts. For example, the Nine Pekinese Swallow (plate 60), takes nine Pekinese with varying expressions as the major theme for the overall picture. The colored ribbons and balls are the parts which bring the Pekinese together and enrich the whole by making it more lively. The design would be less interesting if it failed to include these harmonizing motifs (fig. 82). The Cloud-Crane Eternal Spring Swallow kite is a good

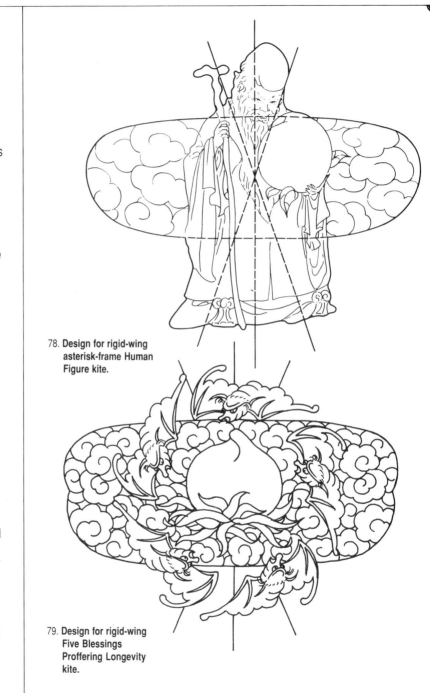

78. **Design for rigid-wing asterisk-frame Human Figure kite.**

79. **Design for rigid-wing Five Blessings Proffering Longevity kite.**

87

example of the whole setting off the parts (plate 64). The entire background consists of rose-colored clouds which delicately contrast each flying crane.

Color. Bright and lustrous colors are used which, when integrated, have an overall striking effect. The coloring of animals is not limited to realism, but is applied for the effect of ideal beauty. For example, the Frog kite and the Bee kite are painted with mineral-based paints so that the pure and translucent colors will glow and glitter when they catch the sun and enhance the hopping or fluttering effect of the kite (plates 78–79). The colors employed on kites take into consideration these three factors: colors used, color application and desired serial effect. Because kite-making is essentially a craft, the colors do not necessarily follow the rules of conventional painting, but are chosen intuitively.

The basic colors are the three primaries: red, yellow and blue. In Chinese folk tradition, the favored colors are red, yellow and green and, less frequently, cool blue. Red, yellow and blue were the main colors of the costumes of the emperor, of most women's clothes and even the embroidered shoes of children in the countryside. Festival verses pasted on either side of main doorways, paper lanterns and so on also use these popular colors. The colors in kite designs are also those of popular folk

handicraft tradition and when applied to an auspicious design make the kite doubly lucky. Suitable warm colors suggesting good fortune and festivity are set off by cool shades (plates 12 and 73).

Black and ultramarine are also frequently used, black as an intermediary color. In traditional Chinese painting, black ink and washes are used to suggest distance and solidity. Although black is commonly used for background contrast, it is also applied as a major decorative color, as on the black and white double swallow kite (plate 82). The surfaces of the heads, tails and wings of these swallows are all black, with only the abdomen left white. Similarly, the main decorative surfaces of the rigid-wing wide swallow kite were originally painted with very bright colors, becoming predominantly blue or black later on. They are called the Black and White Swallow, or *heiguodi*, and the Blue and White Swallow or *languodi* Plump Swallow kites (plates 68—69). In fact, the design of these kites is often more striking in the sky than the beautifully colored designs of the other swallow kites. The effect achieved by using black and white is a contrasting one that is clear in the sky as well as a complete one that can be appreciated for its subtlety and elegance.

Ultramarine is a cool color mostly used for background contrast distributed over large

areas or as an outline color for certain kites. If ultramarine is used, it is generally accompanied by warm colors such as red or orange to make the design rich and vivid. Ultramarine is also used for clouds to set off a human figure or to make a major motif stand out clearly (plate 65).

Techniques for applying color are the second consideration. Traditional realistic painting of figures, birds and so on in China is characterized by several layers of color and close attention to detail, richness of color, elegance and translucence. The technique of applying color to kites is based on this. The brushwork on kites is not so fine as in traditional painting and the process is less detailed, with larger areas of solid color. The desired effect must be clearer and brighter, due to kite's distance from the viewer. Some kites with abundant reds, yellows and greens have a greater folk art flavor. For example, the Longjing Fish kite or the Frog kite have very bold colors with red or green predominant. In sunlight, single areas of red or green reflect countless hues as the kites hop in the sky (plate 72 and 78).

Animal kites may have detailed or simple exaggeration. The Black and White Swallow kite, the Dragonfly and the Longjing Fish kites mentioned above are all examples of simple exaggeration. The Butterfly kite is a good example of striking colors used

80. **Design for flexible-wing Phoenix-Butterfly kite.**

81. **Part of Phoenix-Butterfly kite.**

82. **Part of Nine Pekinese swallow kite.**

83. **Catfish kite "swimming" in the sky.**

with exaggerated details (plates 84–86).

The third factor to be considered when applying color to kites is the degree of contrast between the kite and the sky behind. Against this enormous natural backdrop each kite will appear differently according to design and form. It is always essential to bear in mind the normal tone of the sky and there must be a strong effort to make the colors of the kite stand out clearly in different environments while giving a realistic effect. For example, the catfish twists and glides through the sky when flying, glittering realistically as if swimming in the sea (fig. 83).

New departures may be summed up as follows:

1) Revising the Sand Swallow design. The original Sand Swallow kite was a direct copy of the shape of the swallow, a common bird in China. Over the last hundred years, the form has been modified to the present form (plate 63). The design traditionally includes the eyes, eyebrows, nose and beak;

84. Design of Dragon Guiding His Son.
This unusual design breaks stylized conventions. The picture is placed in the center of the swallow, including the claws and waist sections.

A green dragon looms out of white clouds showing his son, in the lower half, how to puff mist. The combination of clouds, water and dragons works well here.

85. Design of a Hundred-Blessings kite.
The design here is more static than the Dragon Guiding His Son kite: the stylized bats are placed symmetrically over the swallow's body.

Each bat, slightly different in form and expression, seems to wrestle with a golden line. Although tradition calls for a hundred bats, twenty produces a less cluttered, livelier design.

the breast; the feathers on the two wings and tail; and the shoulders formed by small wings. Therefore, the sand swallow kite may be appreciated for both realistic and stylized element. The frame has also undergone continuous modification into today's stylized form of the Chinese kite.

However, the Ha family have not limited themselves to the stylized design. While continuing the traditional form, they have also

become creative in other ways. They retain the conventional arrangement of the head and tail while enlivening the major decoration on the wings, breast and stomach, with a new repertoire of motifs. They have at the same time enriched and enlivened their own kites. Examples of these are the Dragon Guiding His Son, A Hundred Blessings and the Five Fish kites. (figs. 84–86).

2) *Creating new single colors*

and designs. The Catfish kite, for example, has waves of water between its head and tail sections to give the appearance of having just leapt from the sea. Traditionally, the waves are painted red to set off the green of the fish's head or vice versa. Since this can make it appear as if the head and tail are separate when flying, the Has have modified it by using the natural color of the catfish (plate 71).

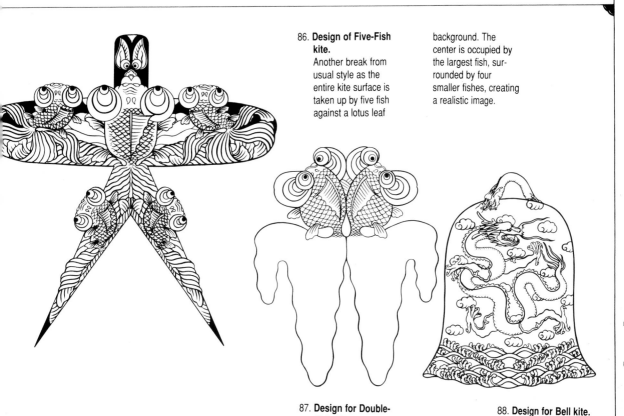

86. Design of Five-Fish kite.
Another break from usual style as the entire kite surface is taken up by five fish against a lotus leaf background. The center is occupied by the largest fish, surrounded by four smaller fishes, creating a realistic image.

87. Design for Double-Fish kite.

88. Design for Bell kite.

Similar modifications have been made on other realistic kites such as the Double Fish, the Bell and the Dragonfly kites, creating realistic designs with few embellishments (figs. 87–88). These kites are largely covered by a few predominant colors (plates 70 and 87). As the great artist Picasso said, "You must understand how to use as few colors as possible. If you have to use seven colors but can make them with two, your skill

is great." The Ha kite-makers have developed this skill while maintaining the pure, rich coloring of traditional Chinese folk art as well.

3) Greater artistic results. The outer skins of all natural forms are shaped by their inner skeletons. With special attention to coordinating between theme and content, design and construction, dominant and subordinate colors, kites have been "sculpted" beautifully

whether seen close at hand or aloft in the sky. For example, the lifelike design of the Phoenix-butterfly kite is detailed with exaggerated colors. The design is a harmonious integration of the Phoenix-butterfly shapes, with a result not only as pleasing as fine painting but a sculptured form which is also a marvelous sight when seen flying and dancing realistically in the sky (plate 86).

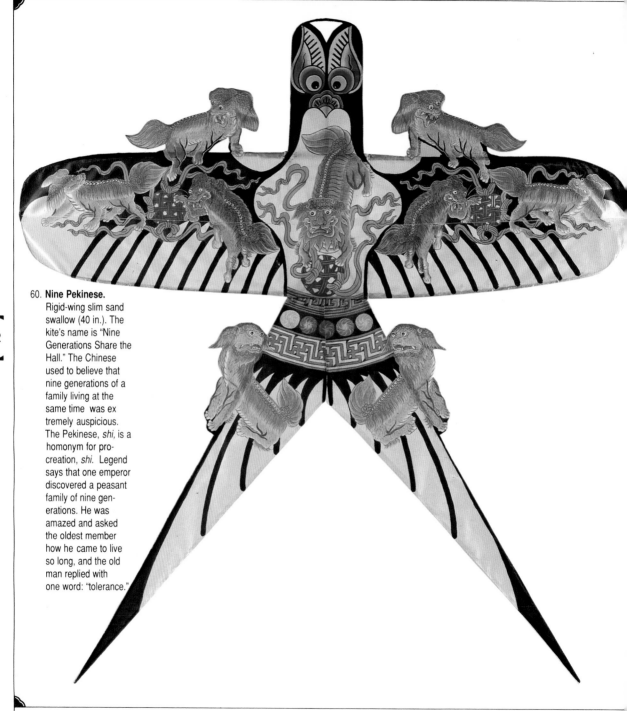

60. **Nine Pekinese.**
Rigid-wing slim sand swallow (40 in.). The kite's name is "Nine Generations Share the Hall." The Chinese used to believe that nine generations of a family living at the same time was ex tremely auspicious. The Pekinese, *shi*, is a homonym for pro-creation, *shi*. Legend says that one emperor discovered a peasant family of nine gen-erations. He was amazed and asked the oldest member how he came to live so long, and the old man replied with one word: "tolerance."

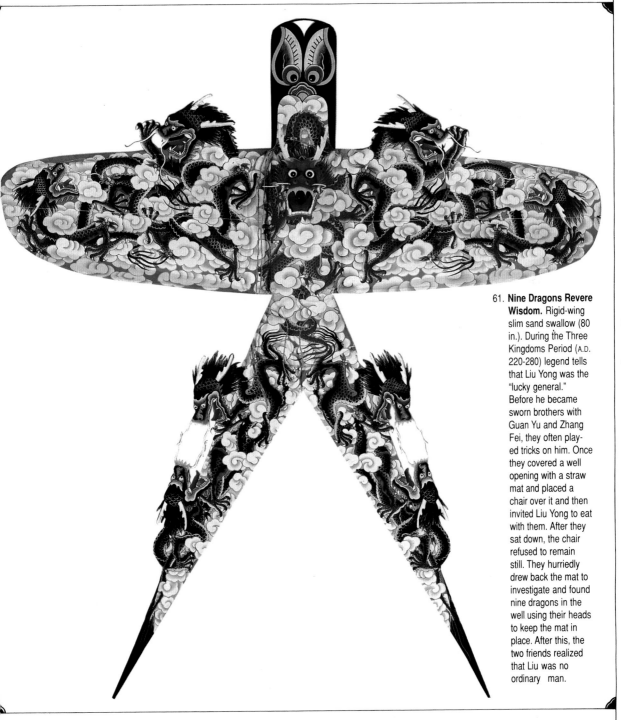

61. **Nine Dragons Revere Wisdom.** Rigid-wing slim sand swallow (80 in.). During the Three Kingdoms Period (A.D. 220-280) legend tells that Liu Yong was the "lucky general." Before he became sworn brothers with Guan Yu and Zhang Fei, they often played tricks on him. Once they covered a well opening with a straw mat and placed a chair over it and then invited Liu Yong to eat with them. After they sat down, the chair refused to remain still. They hurriedly drew back the mat to investigate and found nine dragons in the well using their heads to keep the mat in place. After this, the two friends realized that Liu was no ordinary man.

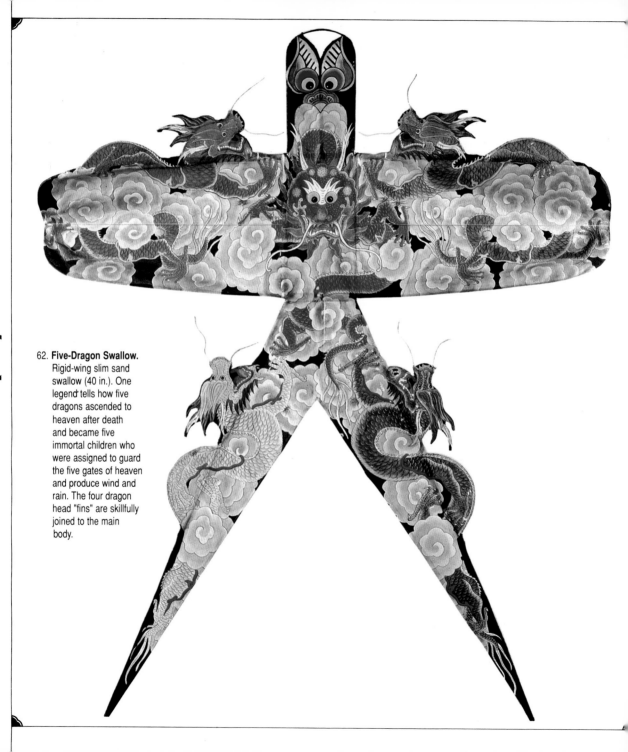

62. **Five-Dragon Swallow.**
Rigid-wing slim sand
swallow (40 in.). One
legend tells how five
dragons ascended to
heaven after death
and became five
immortal children who
were assigned to guard
the five gates of heaven
and produce wind and
rain. The four dragon
head "fins" are skillfully
joined to the main
body.

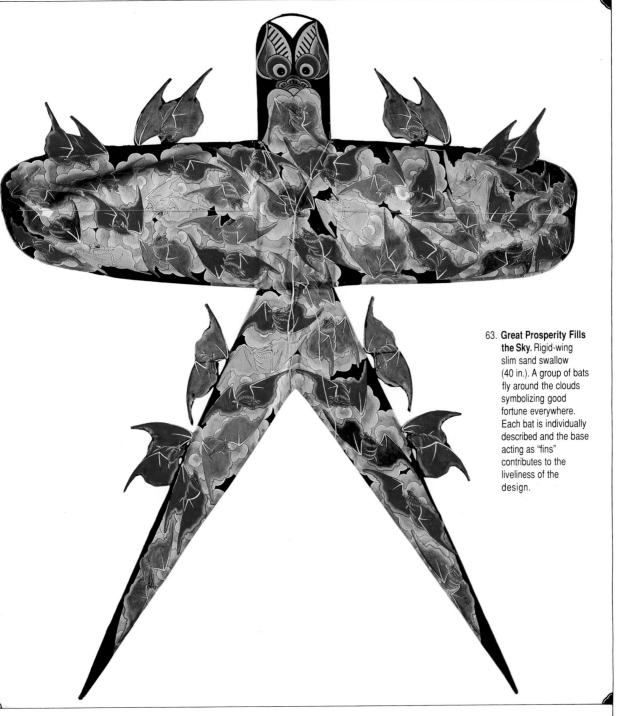

63. **Great Prosperity Fills the Sky.** Rigid-wing slim sand swallow (40 in.). A group of bats fly around the clouds symbolizing good fortune everywhere. Each bat is individually described and the base acting as "fins" contributes to the liveliness of the design.

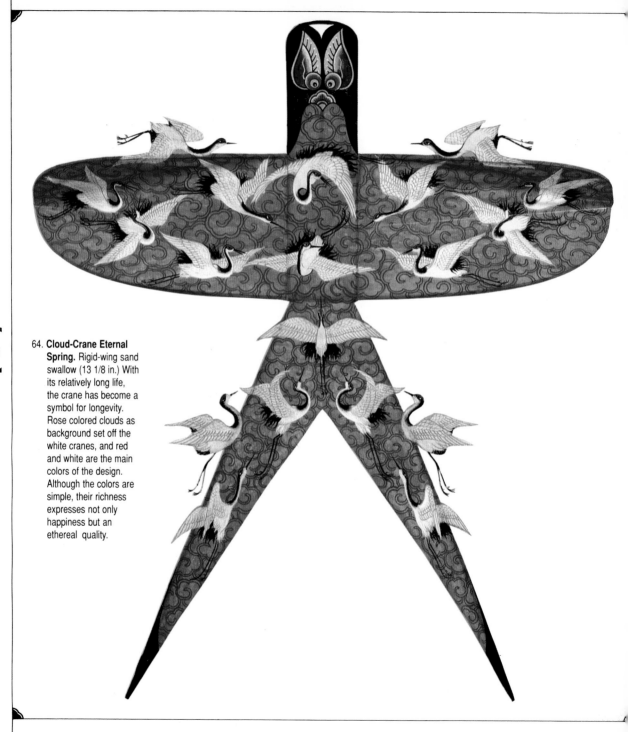

64. **Cloud-Crane Eternal Spring.** Rigid-wing sand swallow (13 1/8 in.) With its relatively long life, the crane has become a symbol for longevity. Rose colored clouds as background set off the white cranes, and red and white are the main colors of the design. Although the colors are simple, their richness expresses not only happiness but an ethereal quality.

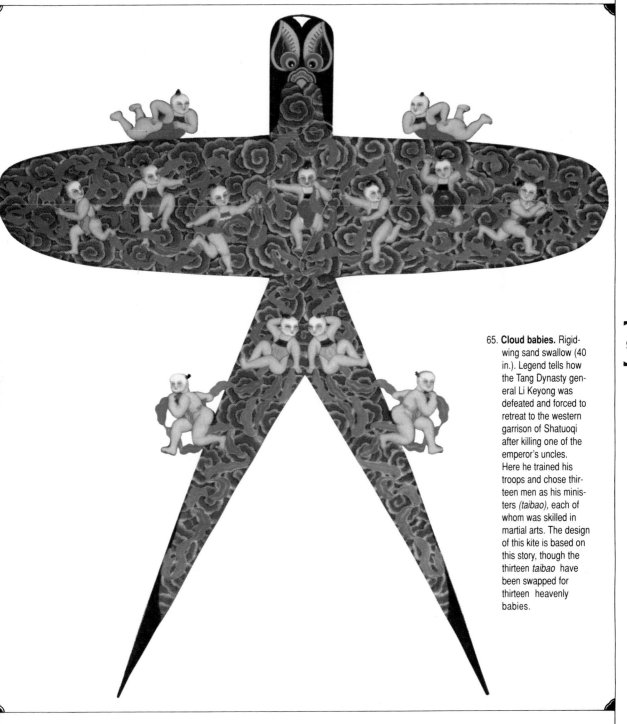

65. **Cloud babies.** Rigid-wing sand swallow (40 in.). Legend tells how the Tang Dynasty general Li Keyong was defeated and forced to retreat to the western garrison of Shatuoqi after killing one of the emperor's uncles. Here he trained his troops and chose thirteen men as his ministers *(taibao),* each of whom was skilled in martial arts. The design of this kite is based on this story, though the thirteen *taibao* have been swapped for thirteen heavenly babies.

66. **Dragon Guiding His Son.** Rigid-wing wide sand swallow (53 1/4 in.). The father dragon is teaching his son how to arise and become an immortal. The red dragon stands astride the mountain and puffs mist as he teaches his son below the water. The design is composed of the dragons, clouds and waves. The red of the dragon's body and the pale red of the clouds provide an area of warm color, while the green waves, the small black dragon and the surrounding blue acts as contrast. The two areas seem to be united by the green mist blown by the large dragon.

67. **A Hundred Blessings.** Rigid-wing wide sand swallow (40 in.). This expresses the wish that auspicious events, like ten thousand horses galloping, will arrive at the same time. A folk song says, "As soon as the new spring is here, everything is right, auspicious as one wish, one hundred blessings arrive like horses." The central decorative area uses blue, red and yellow as the main colors, with green interspersed. Red bats tug at the golden ring and are set off from the cool blue background.

68. **Black and White Swallow.**
Rigid-wing wide sand
swallow (40 in.). The
main design is defined
in black and white.

The white is back-
ground and makes
each part of the
stylized swallow's
body stand out

clearly. Although only
two colors are used,
the design is very
striking when the kite
is flown.

69. **Blue and White
    Swallow.** Rigid-wing
    wide sand swallow (40
    in.). The colors are a
    new variation on the
    black and white
    swallow.

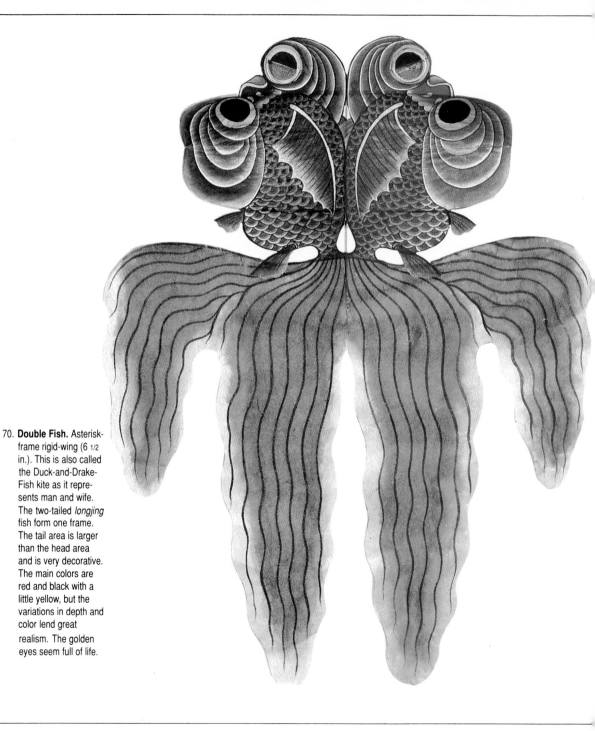

70. **Double Fish.** Asterisk-frame rigid-wing (6 1/2 in.). This is also called the Duck-and-Drake-Fish kite as it represents man and wife. The two-tailed *longjing* fish form one frame. The tail area is larger than the head area and is very decorative. The main colors are red and black with a little yellow, but the variations in depth and color lend great realism. The golden eyes seem full of life.

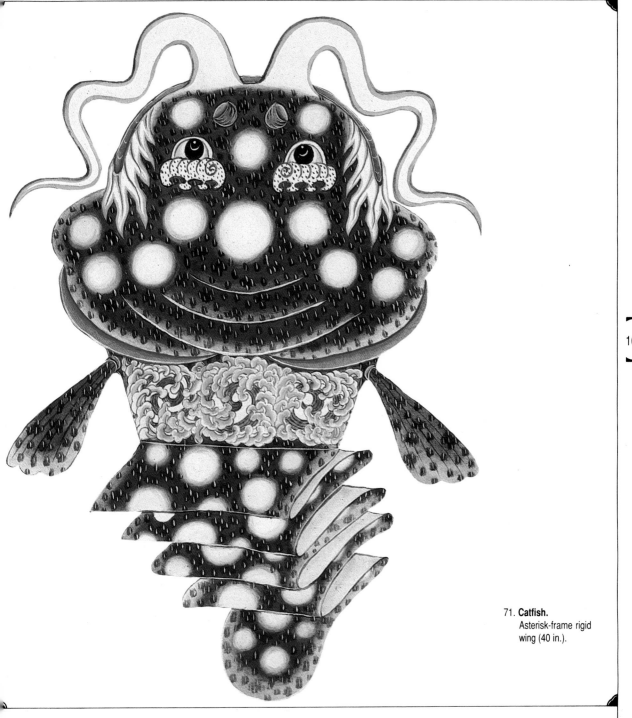

71. **Catfish.**
Asterisk-frame rigid
wing (40 in.).

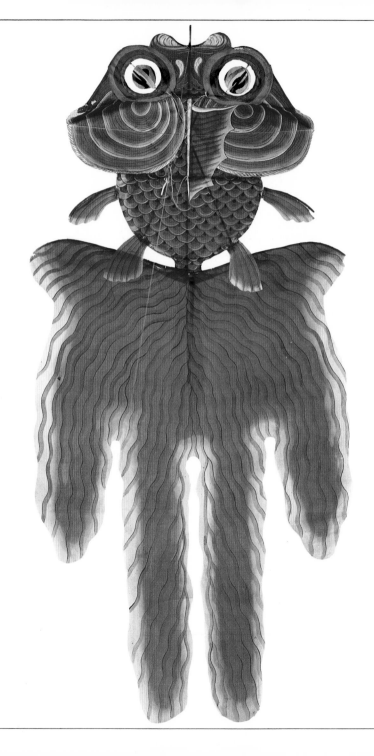

72. **Longjing fish.**
Asterisk -frame rigid-
wing (19 3/4 in.). Based
on the shape of the
longjing fish, the head
and body have a bam-
boo frame, but the tail
is not supported by a
structure. Only one
color is used in addi-
tion to the yellow of
the eyes. When flying,
the eyes roll and the
tail flutters realistically.

73. **Five Blessings Proffering Longevity.** Asterisk-frame rigid-wing (6 5/8 in.). The "five blessings" represent longevity, wealth, health, cultivation of morality, and filial piety. The red bats, five for the five blessings, stand out clearly from the blue background.

74. **Zheng Chenggong.**
Asterisk-frame rigid-
wing (40 in.). Zheng
Cheng-gong (1624–
1662) lived between
the Ming and Qing
dynasties and fought
with the Ming against
the Qing. Because of
his civil and military
skills, he was in-
stalled as lord of
Yanping prefecture,
and was made
general of the forces
opposing the Qing
army. In the fifteenth
year of the reign of
Emperor Yongli
(1661), in response to
appeals of the Tai
wanese he expelled
the Dutch settlers from
the island.

75. **Immortal Maiden He.**
Asterisk-frame rigid-
wing (40 in.). The
Maiden He is one of
the eight immortals
of Taoism. During the
Tang Dynasty
(618–907), she was
the daughter of Gover-
nor He of Cengcheng
County, Guandong
Province. At fourteen,
she dreamt a spirit
showed her how to eat
a kind of powder to
achieve immortality.
Then she woke. She
vowed never to marry
and would frequently drift
like a cloud among hills and
valleys. Later, she stopped
eating staple food alto-
gether, and became an
immortal in the Jinglong
Period (707—710).

76. **Five Boys Playing Round a General.** Asterisk-frame rigid-wing (40 in.). Five boys are trying to snatch the helmet. Helmet, *kui,* and general, *kui,* are homonyms. The embroidered helmet represents the definite attainment of official rank, or more specifically, the actual rank of general.

77. **Melon Butterfly.** Double-layered rigid-wing (5 1/4 in.). With its wings pointed upwards and downwards, this kite requires skillful manufacture. The design is based around a melon split into quarters.

78. **Green Dragonfly.**
Double-layered rigid-wing
(6 1/2 in.). See text to
plate 21.

79. **Bee.** Multi-layered rigid-
wing (6 1/2 in.). A realistic
and straightforward design
using three layers, the upper and lower wings and
the abdomen.

80. **Frog.** Multi-layered rigid-wing (6 1/2 in.). Using three layers, this kite looks poised to hop forward. The design relies on simple exaggeration, and most of the surface is covered with a clear, translucent green with circles outlined in dark green to enhance the realistic effect.

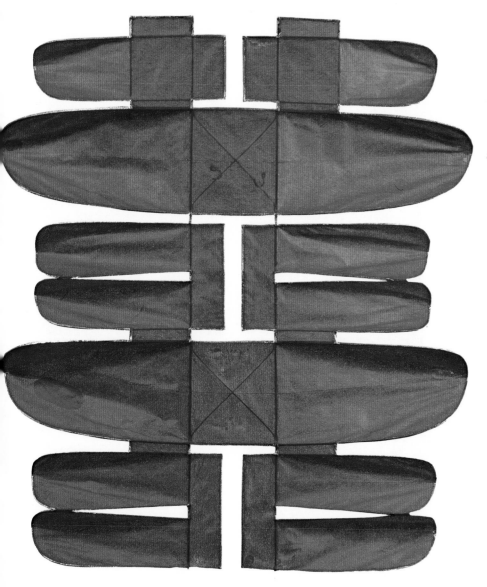

81. **Double Happiness.**
Multiple-layered rigid wing
(13 1/8 in.). Made with
several layers, the frame
reveals clearly the shape
of the character. Because
each layer helps lift the
kite, no single part is
purely decorative.

113

82. **Two Black and White Swallows.** Single-layer flexible wing (13 1/8). The design is highly realistic. The two swallows are suspended at either end of a connecting pole and one string is tied to the center. When flying, the pole moves and bends easily in the wind, making the swallows dance and flutter around each other.

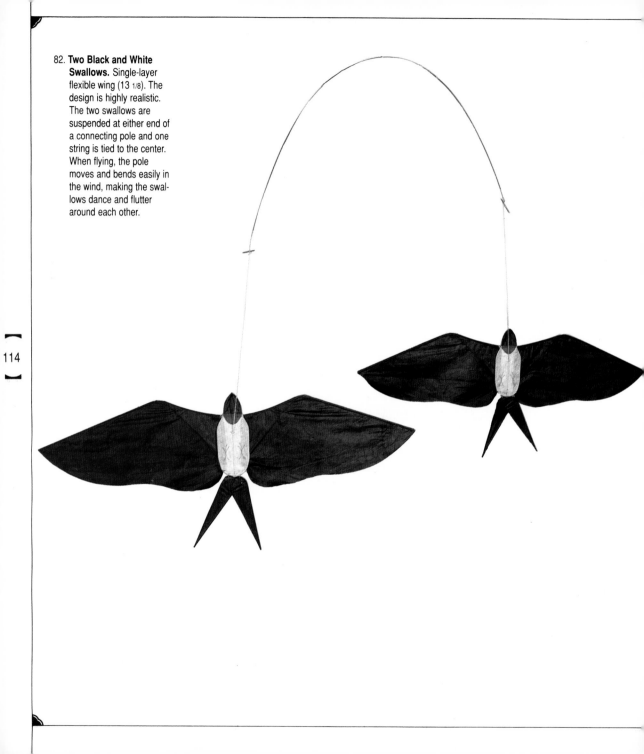

83. **Bat.**
Single-layered flexible-
wing (40 in.). Like a
combination of good
fortune and longevity
kites. The exaggerated
red body of the bat sets
off the green leaves of
the immortal peaches.
The bright red and
green are favored
folk colors.

84. **Colored Butterfly.**
Double-layered flexible-
wing (40 in.). The
surface of the kite is
composed of rainbow
colors radiating out-
ward. The careful de-
sign has both a popular
and a regal appear-
ance.

85. **Fish Butterfly.**
Double-layered flexible-
wing (40 in.). The body
of the butterfly is like a
fish, but the kite is
butterfly-shaped. The
choice and contrast of
colors is subtly
conceived.

86. **Phoenix Butterfly.**
Double-layered flexible-
wing (53 1/4 in.).
Realistic but with a riot
of phoenix colors, the
decorative parts are
especially well inte-
grated and joined to
the main kite body. The
contrasting colors are
based on carpet de-
signs and the result is
vibrant.

87. Bell.
Rigid-wing square-frame (40 in.). Design is based on the huge bell in Beijing's Bell Temple. The mythical beast on top is a *pulao*, like a dragon but with a smaller body. Both it and the dragon playing with a pearl on the main surface have gaping mouths. The subtle colors suggest the ancient bronze of the original bell.

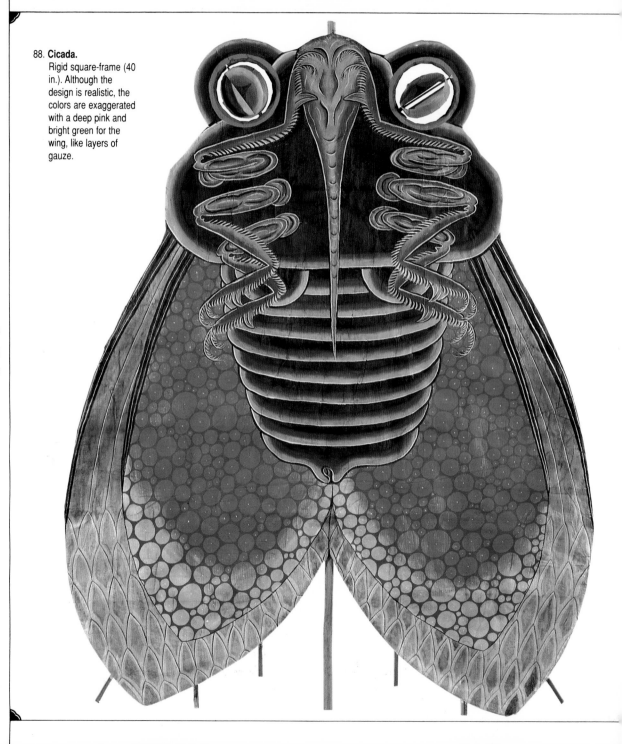

88. **Cicada.**
Rigid square-frame (40 in.). Although the design is realistic, the colors are exaggerated with a deep pink and bright green for the wing, like layers of gauze.

89. **Bi-Colored Rhombus.**
Soft-flap (13 1/8in.) One
of the earliest and
simplest designs, often
called the *pilian* kite.

90. **Chang E Rising Up to the Moon.** Umbrella-wing (40 in.). Tradition says that the goddess Chang E was the wife of Hou Yi. Hou managed to convince the Goddess Mother of the West, Xiwangmu, to give him the elixir of life, but Chang E secretly drank it and after floating up to the moon became its deity.

91. **Monkey King.**
Umbrella-wing (40 in.).
This is Sun Wukong, the
monkey king from the
Chinese classic, *Journey
to the West.* Brave and
bold, he knows seventy-
two forms of magic. After
discovering the beauti-
ful Waterfall Cave of
the Mount of Flower and
Fruit, he moved with his
band of monkey followers
and established himself
as the Monkey King.

124

92.**Heavenly Maiden Scatters Flowers.**
Umbrella wing (40 in.). A Buddhist scripture describes how bodhisattvas and disciples are tested by a heavenly maid. When a flower falls on a bodhisattva, it will slip off. But if it doesn't fall off a disciple, then it means that the disciple hasn't cultivated himself enough. Petals falling down create a snow-like scene.

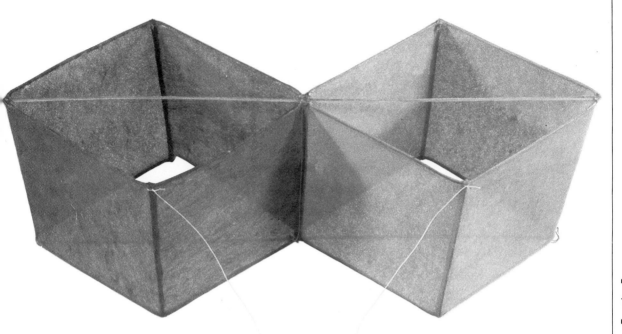

93. **Double Rhombus.**
   Three-dimensional (13 1/8
   in.). Relatively simple in
   design and construction.
   An easy flier.

Chapter

4

Kite-Making:

Methods

and

Procedure

The first thing to consider when making kites is the selection and preparation of the materials. Most kite frames use bamboos of various ages and thicknesses, reeds, or wooden strips (fig. 89). Thin dowels may also be used. Wood or dowels may be substituted for bamboo where it is not readily available. Binding materials include hemp, cotton, paper string and paper strips (figs. 90–91). Gluing agents include various types of paste and chemical gums. The kite covers may be made of oil-paper, *xuan* paper (a high quality paper made in Xuancheng), *anhui* paper (often used for traditional Chinese painting), high strength paper, cotton-fiber paper, silk of varying strength, hard surface paper and cotton. Paint materials include mineral pigment types or alkaline paints (for their translucence), water colors and traditional Chinese painting colors (fig. 92).

The basic tools for kite-making include: scissors, pliers, pincers, a stove, a spirit lamp or candle, files, fine-toothed saws, large and small knives, an iron and an ironing board, single and double handled planes, brushes, ink, ink grinders as well as various needles and drills (figs. 93–95).

First select the framing material. The major parts of the kite frame use comparatively firm bamboo canes up to one year old while the decorative parts are made with younger bamboos. The firm bamboo ensures that the frame will retain its shape after binding, while the

89. **Various bamboo canes and struts.**

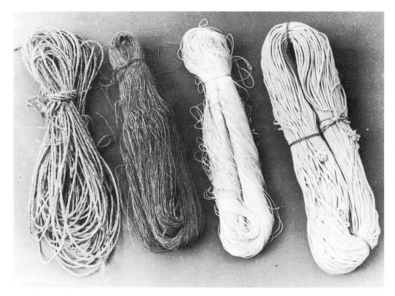

90. **Binding materials (1).**

91. **Binding materials (2).**

92. **Paint materials.**

93. **Tools (1).**

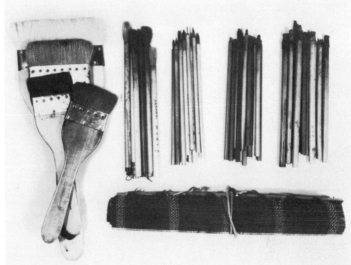

94. **Tools (2).**

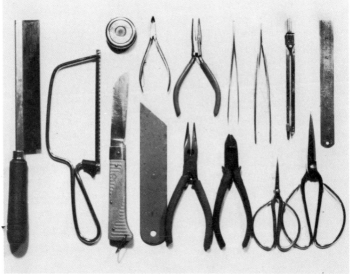

95. **Tools (3).**

129

supple bamboo is easy to bend and bow into the correct shape. Before binding it is very important to ascertain first the strength, thickness and length of the bamboos needed for the main frame and for the subsidiary parts.

In binding the frame there are several basic procedures for shaving and joining the struts. *Shaving* is achieved by 1) paring by pulling (fig. 96); 2) paring by pushing (fig. 97); 3) planing (fig. 98); 4) whittling (fig. 99); 5) filing (fig. 100). *Joining* is accomplished by 1) kneeling and binding (fig. 101); 2) pairing and binding (fig.102); 3) inserting (fig. 103); and overlapping splice (fig. 104).

Each kite has a different binding process:

Rigid-Wing. 1) The Sand Swallow kite has three separate parts, the head, wings and legs. Its flight relies on the elasticity and forward curve of the two wings. The three parts of the whole kite have a strength ratio of 7:3:2. For the top edge of the wing, two bamboo canes of equal length and strength should be shaved down by paring or planing and then joined with an overlapping joint (fig. 105). The two parts should fit together precisely. Use the same method for the bottom edge of the wing. The wingspan of a Sand Swallow under 40 inches is generally considered as short and the corresponding lengths of the top and bottom edges of the wing can be gauged at a glance so a single bamboo cane can be used

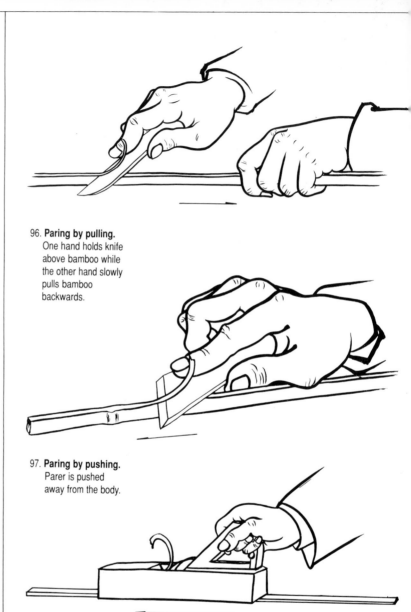

96. **Paring by pulling.** One hand holds knife above bamboo while the other hand slowly pulls bamboo backwards.

97. **Paring by pushing.** Parer is pushed away from the body.

98. **Planing.** Always plane forward.

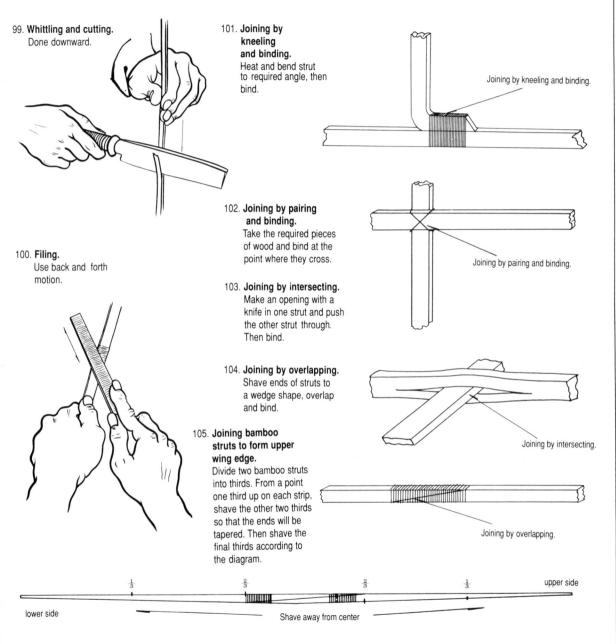

99. Whittling and cutting.
Done downward.

100. Filing.
Use back and forth
motion.

**101. Joining by
kneeling
and binding.**
Heat and bend strut
to required angle, then
bind.

Joining by kneeling and binding.

**102. Joining by pairing
and binding.**
Take the required pieces
of wood and bind at the
point where they cross.

Joining by pairing and binding.

103. Joining by intersecting.
Make an opening with a
knife in one strut and push
the other strut through.
Then bind.

104. Joining by overlapping.
Shave ends of struts to
a wedge shape, overlap
and bind.

Joining by intersecting.

**105. Joining bamboo
struts to form upper
wing edge.**
Divide two bamboo struts
into thirds. From a point
one third up on each strip,
shave the other two thirds
so that the ends will be
tapered. Then shave the
final thirds according to
the diagram.

Joining by overlapping.

$\frac{1}{3}$ $\frac{2}{3}$ $\frac{2}{3}$ $\frac{1}{3}$ upper side

lower side

Shave away from center

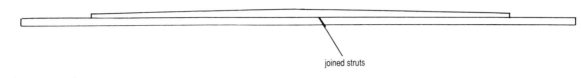

joined struts

106. Extra strut for strength

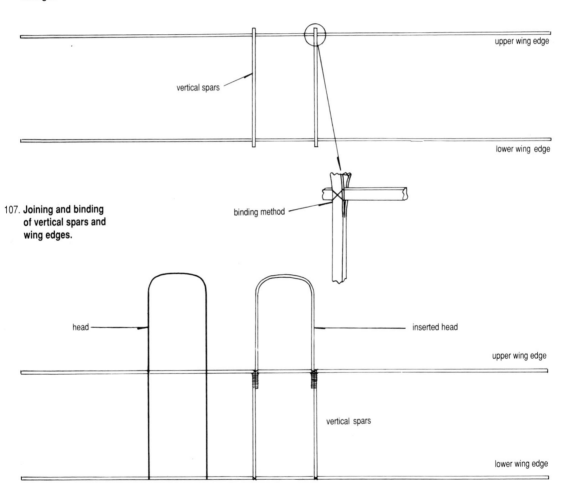

upper wing edge

vertical spars

lower wing edge

107. Joining and binding of vertical spars and wing edges.

binding method

head

inserted head

upper wing edge

vertical spars

lower wing edge

108. Binding for head section complete.

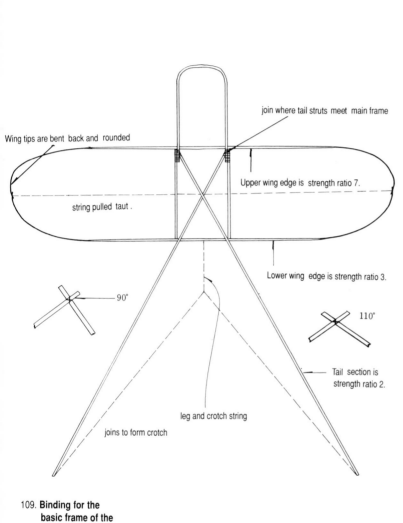

Wing tips are bent back and rounded

join where tail struts meet main frame

Upper wing edge is strength ratio 7.

string pulled taut .

Lower wing edge is strength ratio 3.

90°

110°

Tail section is strength ratio 2.

leg and crotch string

joins to form crotch

109. **Binding for the basic frame of the Sand Swallow kite.**

instead of two. For a wingspan over 40 inches, the method of joining two bamboos, as in fig.105, should be used. This will guarantee that both sides are roughly equal and also helps reinforce the central part. For kites with comparatively large measurements, it is necessary to use more than one bamboo cane for the wings and glue them inside to inside (fig. 106). When this is done, both bamboo strips must be shaved according to the method above to increase the strength of the wings.

When the main frame and subsidiary parts have been shaved according to the 7:3:2 ratio, they can be bound together.

First, select two firm strips of shaved bamboo for the supporting struts and use the joining-by-inserting method to bind the top and bottom edges together (fig.107) with a length of string. The two struts are important parts of the frame and support the wing section. Because this is the main area of wind resistance these parts must be securely bound together.

Next, the head and "fins" must be bound to the frame. The lower part of the head is bound to the frame between the two supporting struts using the joining-by-inserting method (fig.108). (If the supporting struts are under 40 inches long, use the same bamboo cane for the head. If they are longer, then the head must be inserted as described above). Then take the ends of the top and bottom edges and bind them together with the joining-by-

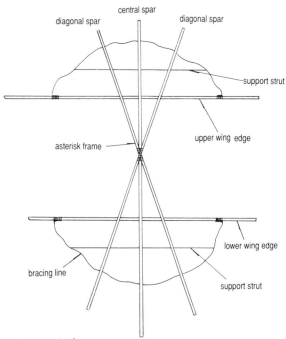

110. **Binding for basic asterisk frame.**

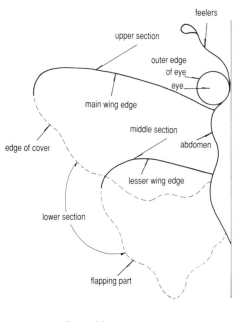

111. **Parts of the Butterfly kite frame.**

inserting method at an angle of 90° or 110°. Tie the right and left tips of the two wings together and secure them firmly to the supporting struts in the middle. This will give the wings their characteristic date-stone shape (fig.109).

Finally, bind the two "legs." The top ends of the bamboo struts should be inserted at the point where they meet the top wing edge, then paired and bound where it crosses the lower wing edge. Although the two legs are both tied to the frame in the same way, one may bend out while the other bends in. To avoid this, both legs can be bent equally forward or backward by heating. Next, form the inside of the legs and the crotch with one length of string. Tie two ends securely to the ends of the legs, cross them at the crotch and then tie the ends to the bottom wing edge between the supporting struts. If it is too tight, then the legs will bend inwards; if too slack, then the string will be un-even. This is the complete frame for the Sand Swallow (fig. 109).

The asterisk-frame kite is another rigid frame design. To construct it, first shave the bamboos proportionally for the main parts and begin binding. Begin with the central spar and bind it to the exact center of the top and bottom wing edge. Then bind the diagonal spars at the point where they cross the central spar in the center (fig. 110). Next, join the ends of the top and bottom wing edges by intersecting and binding. To make the date-stone shape and curve the tips of the wings, tie a string at the right tip and stretch it across to the left wing tip and bind together. Each different design has varying decorative parts which can be molded into shape by heating and then joining to the frame. Caution is necessary at this point. A kite with a wingspan of over

134

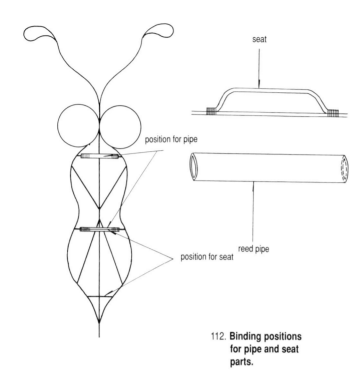

seat

position for pipe

reed pipe

position for seat

112. **Binding positions for pipe and seat parts.**

tance. It will also reduce the friction between the air current and the kite, which will in turn affect the balance of the lift, weight and pressure that keeps the kite in the air.

When shaving the bamboos for the main and lesser wings, begin a third from the end of each bamboo and slowly work towards both ends so that the ends will be thinner and more flexible and the middle stronger. Then make a triangular-shaped support for the main wing by binding the top ends of two struts two-fifths along the top left and right edges of the main wings and binding the lower ends to the support spar (fig. 37). This will increase the strength of the inside edge of the wings, and will also insure that the other parts of the kite retain their shape. A similar triangular-shaped support should be made for the smaller wings. Because these wings' main functions are to control the wind current and stabilize the kite, a small area should extend below the butterfly's lesser wings like a rudder.

Rigid Square-Frame. This kite is flat, with a construction procedure similar to other kites. The bell kite is made from several major bamboo struts (fig. 39): one strut for the central spar, two for the two subordinate spars running parallel on either side of the central spar, two for the cross spars and two for the diagonal spars. Comparatively thin bamboos or reeds should be used to cover the hollow center. These should be bound together so that when the frame is finished the

13 inches will take a greater wind force, making it necessary to bind one or more supporting strips to the outline frame and the wings, according to the design. The shape for the binding support is usually a triangular, horizontal or vertical arrangement (fig. 110).

Flexible-Wing. The Butterfly kite frame is divided into the upper, middle and lower sections (fig. 111). The upper section is the top edge of the main wing, the middle section is the top edge of the lesser wing, and the lower section consists of the bottom edges of the main and lesser wings which are the flexible

part of the kite.

To build the frame, bend the bamboo struts into the necessary shapes and bind them together. Take the pipe (reed or bamboo) and the seat of the fixed wing sections and bind these at the predetermined points (fig. 112). Then make the wings. The main wing is a crucial part. To resemble a real butterfly's wing, the top edge must incline outwards. However, according to aerodynamic principles, the main wing cannot be too high and should remain level with the butterfly's eye (see fig. 111). If it is too high, it will reduce the kite's area of wind resis-

entire surface will be chequered and outlined with a bamboo perimeter.

Firmness, smoothness and light weight are crucial to a kite of this kind. The main spars must be strong and securely bound. The surface must be absolutely smooth and even. If the main frame is strong, then lighter spars can be used to span the hollow center.

After gluing on the pointed kite cover, two tasseled tails may be tied to the frame. This insures pull against high winds and stability, and also a smoother landing for the kite. The length of the string or ribbon will affect the kite differently in different winds, so it should be adjusted before flying. If there is a high wind, then the tail should be lengthened, and vice versa.

Flexible Square-Frame. The Eight Trigrams kite has a six-point asterisk frame with four crossing spars and uses eight struts to make two square shapes. When overlapping the asterisk, these struts will make an eight-pointed star, the basic frame (fig. 113). The strongest part of the frame will be the middle crossing point of the central and side spars of the asterisk part, and the weakest part will be the horizontal spars and the eight struts around the edges. After gluing on the cover, tie a length of string to one end of the horizontal spar to make the kite body curve outward (fig. 41). Next, tie two lengths of string to the lower two points on either side of the diagonal spars,

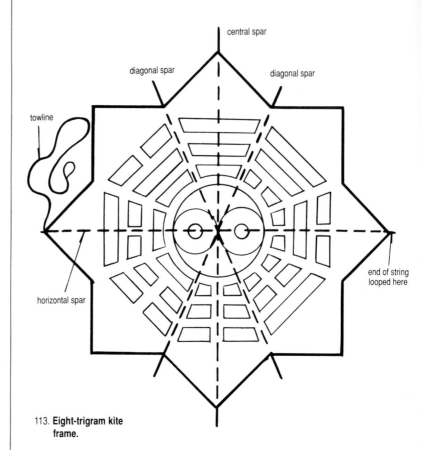

113. **Eight-trigram kite frame.**

then tie them together to form a long tail.

Soft-Flap. The Pot-shaped kite has a frame made with three bamboo struts that cross over one horizontal spar (fig. 43). After gluing on the cover, attach two long tassels to the two points on either side of the pot "bottom" and another in the middle. There may be slight variations in the shape of this kite

depending on the design.

Multi-Layered. The Dragon-headed Centipede kite is made from ten to several hundred round (or other shapes) of rigid-flap or semi-rigid-flap kites strung together in succession. The first flap must be very strong as it not only carries the head design, but also leads the body behind it. The more layers that are added, the stronger the head

114. **Construction of a section, *guangr*, of multi-layered kite.** The length of the vertical spar must not be greater than the diameter of the circle. The horizontal spar is four times the diameter. Shave the horizontal spar away from the point where it meets the circle on each end.

115. **Back view of half-frame section.**

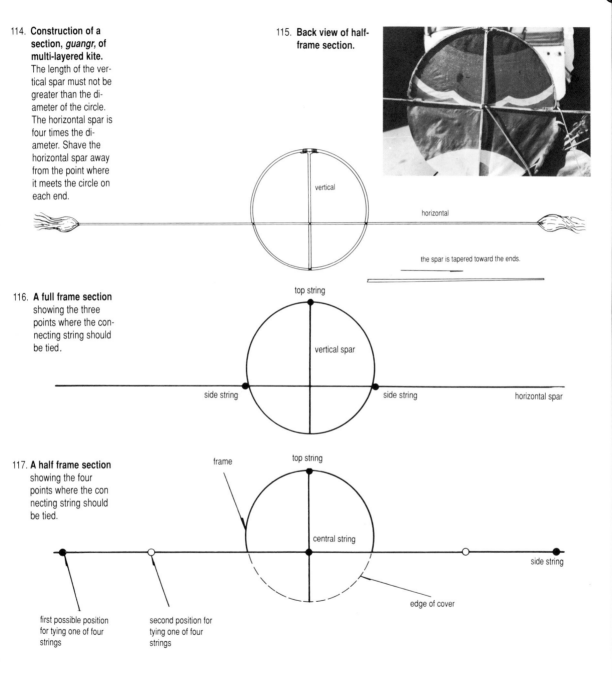

vertical

horizontal

the spar is tapered toward the ends.

116. **A full frame section** showing the three points where the connecting string should be tied.

top string

vertical spar

side string

side string

horizontal spar

117. **A half frame section** showing the four points where the connecting string should be tied.

frame

top string

central string

side string

edge of cover

first possible position for tying one of four strings

second position for tying one of four strings

must be.

The frame of the actual dragon's head must be carefully prepared for both strength and realism. The inside should be reinforced with a cross-shaped frame and the points for attaching string, including the nose, must also be reinforced. They must be firm and the lines must be very securely tied.

Next, make the frames of the centipede. There are two types of frames, the full and the half. The full frame is formed by heating bamboo and bending it into a round shape, then binding the two ends together (fig. 114). The half-frame is a bamboo bent into a semicircle, then paired and bound to a firm horizontal spar (fig. 115). Feathers or tassels may be tied to both ends of the horizontal spar. These help stabilize the kite and serve as "feet" of the centipede.

The centipede segments must be strung together with extreme care for optimum appearance and flying performance. There are two methods for tying. One is to have three strings running from the dragon's head and tied to each full frame at the following three points: the top part of the central spar and on either side where the frame meets the horizontal spar (fig. 115). The other method is to tie the half frame at four points: the top of the central spar, the point where the central spar crosses the horizontal spar, and at both ends of the horizontal spar or in the middle (fig. 117).

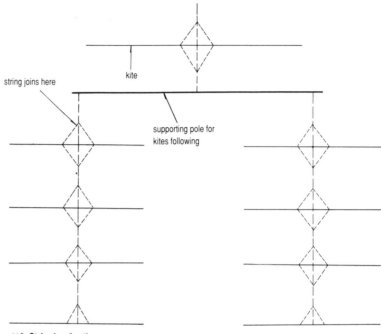

118. **Stringing for the Geese-in-V-Formation kite.**

When stringing the half-frames together, it is important to 1) tie a firm knot so that the frames are securely fastened and 2) insure that the distance between each frame is twice the diameter of the frame itself and 3) make the distance between each frame exactly equal.

The Geese-in-V-Formation is composed of any number of flexible-wing geese kites strung together to fly in V-formation like the real birds. As with the Dragon Centipede kite, the first goose must have a strong frame to pull and lead the geese behind. This requires a strong spar to carry two lines of geese from either

end. When stringing together the geese, use three strings, but join them as one string between each goose (fig. 118).

Umbrella-Wing and Soft-Flap. The top part of this kite looks like a two-dimensional umbrella, and the bottom part is a rectangular-shaped soft-flap. The two parts are joined by the central spar of the frame, which resembles an umbrella handle. This "umbrella handle" and the sloping sides of the umbrella are the strongest points of the frame, while the supporting struts between are weaker. The bamboo struts for the three supports of the rectangular

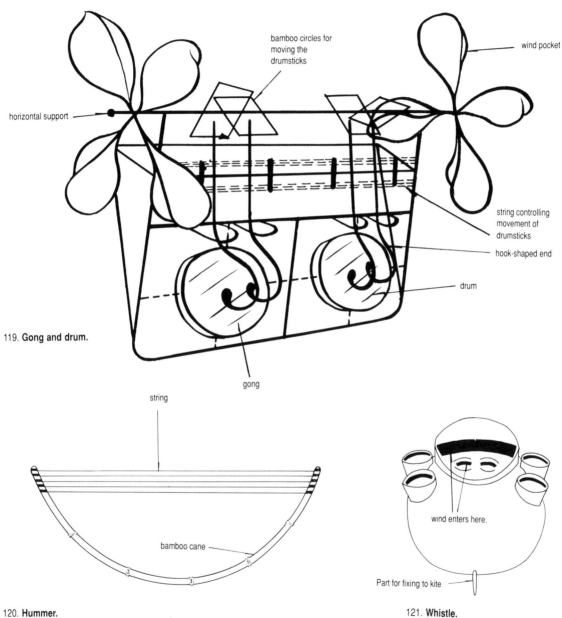

bamboo circles for
moving the
drumsticks

wind pocket

horizontal support

string controlling
movement of
drumsticks

hook-shaped end

drum

119. **Gong and drum.**

gong

string

120. **Hummer.**

bamboo cane

121. **Whistle.**

wind enters here.

Part for fixing to kite

139

flap are the least sturdy parts. A string should be attached to one end of each of these struts and a loop formed at the other end of the string to be hooked to the corresponding end of the strut to bow the umbrella like a keel when flying (fig. 49).

Three-Dimensional Kites. The Double-Bucket kite is composed of three bamboo circles and eight firm bamboo struts are required for each of the buckets. The bamboo struts should be one-and-a-half to two times the diameter of the bamboo circles in length. Begin by making one bucket. Heat and bend three bamboos and bind the ends to form three circles. Place the eight bamboo sticks evenly around the sides of the bamboo circles to form the bucket frame. Four struts placed equidistant act as the main frame support while four thinner struts placed equidistant support the cover. The bamboo circles should also be spaced evenly at the top, center and bottom. After this, construct the second bucket and bind the two together. Finally, heat a slender bamboo to curve slightly and bind this across the top of the two buckets to form the "yoke" (fig. 51).

When making a larger double-bucket kite, it is necessary to add a cross-shaped or asterisk-shaped support fixed horizontally in the middle of each bucket to support the eight struts running vertically on the outside. A cross placed vertically in

the center can also be used for further support.

Kite accessories are decorative additions, made in many forms. Following are a few of many types:

1) Gong and Drum (fig. 119). Bind the gong and drum (approximately 4 inches in diameter) to a bracket formed by binding relatively strong bamboo struts into a tapered V-shape. Make four drumsticks by curving the ends of four bamboos and bind them in the correct place to the bracket. The horizontal strut of the bracket (called the moving axle) should have two windmills at each end, each windmill with four pockets. Next, affix four rectangular bamboo rings to the axle to complete the gong and drum.

2) The Hummer (fig. 120). Heat a bamboo cane to form a bow and stretch three to five strings of silk or similar material in a row across and tie firmly to both ends. The hummer is usually attached to the backs of rigid square-frame kites or sand swallows.

3) The Whistle (fig. 121). Made from gourds, reed pipes or bamboo.

4) The Food-Sender or "Hurrier" (fig. 122). This kite is called the food-sender because it climbs the tow line when wind catches it, hurrying up the towline sending food to the kite. The food-sender has two wings like a butterfly to catch the wind. Attached is a rectangular box filled with scraps of paper. When flying the kite, hook the string from the food-sender's frame to the end

of the flexible bamboo tail. This will open the wings. Then attach the food-sender to the towline with wire and it will rise up the line. When it reaches the kite it will stop, but because it is still catching the wind, the string will slip off the end of the bamboo tail, the wings will close and the food-sender will return down the towline. The moving lid of the box will open and the little colored pieces of paper will be scattered across the sky like flowers.

5) Blinking Eye (fig.123). This kite is circular with two wind-boxes. Make the circle with a bamboo slat or a piece of cardboard. Glue a semicircular piece of card to either side of the circle to prevent the wind from passing through directly. This insures that both sides will bulge outward when they catch the wind, like an eye.

6) The Spiraller (fig.124). There are three types; the first has two spirals facing downwards, the second has two spirals crosswise and the third has spirals like a windmill. Each type is glued to the kite. The spirals must rotate in the same direction.

Gluing. There are four basic gluing techniques, one or more of which may be used in construction: 1) gluing the cover flat (fig. 125); 2) turning the hem of the cover and gluing (fig. 126); 3) gluing at certain points only; 4) gluing extra squares of paper or cloth as reinforcement.

The wings of the rigid-wing kites curve backwards in an arc shape.

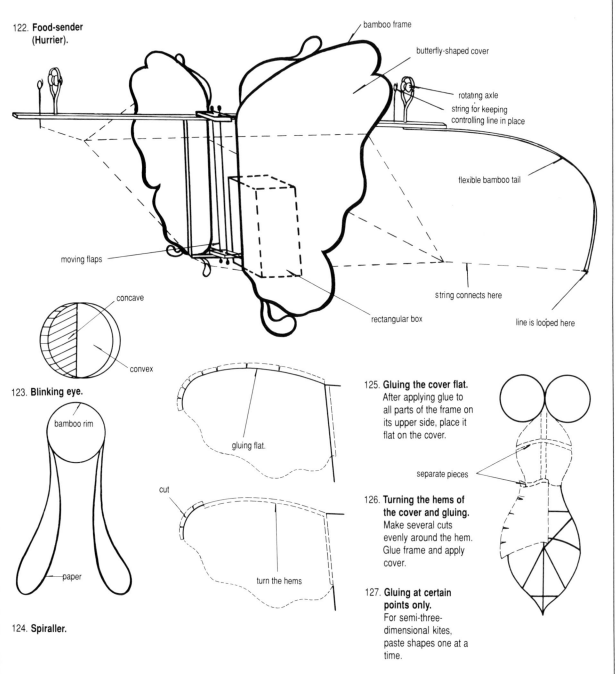

122. **Food-sender (Hurrier).**

bamboo frame

butterfly-shaped cover

rotating axle

string for keeping controlling line in place

flexible bamboo tail

moving flaps

string connects here

rectangular box

line is looped here

concave

convex

123. **Blinking eye.**

bamboo rim

paper

124. **Spiraller.**

gluing flat.

cut

turn the hems

125. **Gluing the cover flat.**
After applying glue to all parts of the frame on its upper side, place it flat on the cover.

separate pieces

126. **Turning the hems of the cover and gluing.**
Make several cuts evenly around the hem. Glue frame and apply cover.

127. **Gluing at certain points only.**
For semi-three-dimensional kites, paste shapes one at a time.

When gluing, first make a small, inch-long nick on one side of the paper you want to glue to the frame. The paper should be applied from behind the wing so that it can stretched smoothly. Spread the glue on the frame. Place the frame flat face downwards. With the thumb of one hand press the cover firmly onto the central area of the wing where the spars cross, and with the other thumb press on the area where the wing tips meet the cover. After gluing it flat, leave a proportionate margin around the sides of paper, fold it over the frame and glue it down. The gluing process for the flexible-wing kites and all others is basically the same. However, reinforcements of silk or paper should be applied around bulges, corners, curves and central parts of the back.

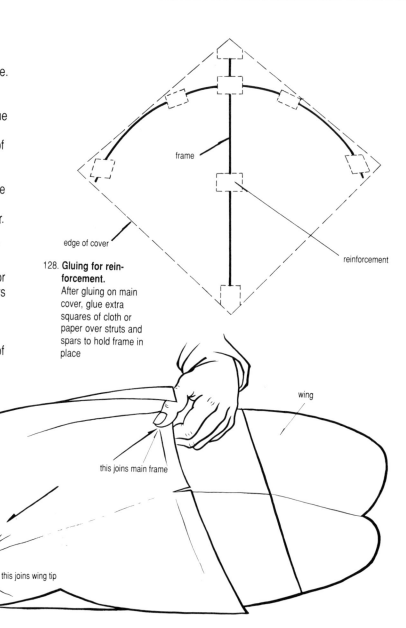

128. **Gluing for reinforcement.**
After gluing on main cover, glue extra squares of cloth or paper over struts and spars to hold frame in place

frame

edge of cover

reinforcement

cloth

wing

this joins main frame

this joins wing tip

129. **Basic method for gluing cover to wing of rigid-wing kites.**

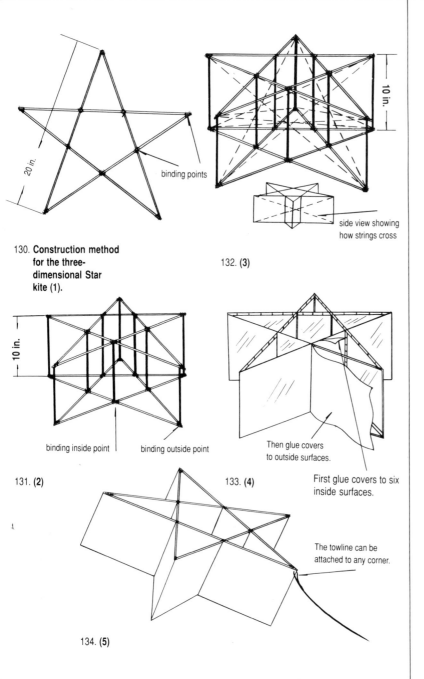

330 in.

binding points

130. **Construction method for the three-dimensional Star kite (1).**

10 in.

side view showing how strings cross

132. **(3)**

10 in.

binding inside point   binding outside point

131. **(2)**

Then glue covers to outside surfaces.

First glue covers to six inside surfaces.

133. **(4)**

The towline can be attached to any corner.

134. **(5)**

Constructing the Three-Dimensional Star Kite

1) Take ten pieces of bamboo, approximately 1/8" x 1/8" x 20" and straighten them by heating over a candle or spirit lamp. Then bind them to make two flat, star-shaped frames (fig.130).

2) Take ten pieces of bamboo 1/8" x 1/8" x10" and use these to join the five outside points and five inside points of the two star frames. The two frames should be ten inches apart (fig. 131).

3) With strong string, tie each corner of the kite to the corresponding opposite corner.

4) When the frame is completed, use comparatively thin yet strong colored paper to cover it and use paste to glue it down. First, glue the five inside corners and then the five outside (fig. 133).

5) Tie a towline to any one of the five outside corners (fig.134).

143

Constructing the Rigid-Wing Butterfly Kite

1) Prepare the main wing, using two pieces of bamboo. For the top edge of the wing, the bamboo should be 1 3/8" x 1/ 5/8" x 26". The bottom edge should be 1" x 1 5/8" x 26". Shave down both ends of the bamboos, cutting away from the center so that they remain thicker in the middle. Shave the top and bottom wing edges to different thicknesses (fig. 135).

2) Take three bamboos measuring 3/16" x 1/8" x 19" to form the central and diagonal spars. Bind these spars at all points where they meet the top and bottom wing edges of the butterfly's main wing. Bind the central spar first (fig. 136).

3) Cross over and bind each of the ends of the top and bottom wing edges. Tie a string from one to another, winding it around the central spar for extra strength (fig. 137), giving the wing the characteristic date-stone shape.

4) Take two bamboo struts measuring 1/4" x 1/8" x 18" and bow them by heating into the required shapes for the lesser wing, the head and the antennae of the butterfly (fig. 138).

5) Split these parts with a knife (fig. 139).

6) Bind these parts to their positions on the main wing, then cut off the parts of the central and diagonal spars that protrude beyond the frame. The frame is now basically complete.

144

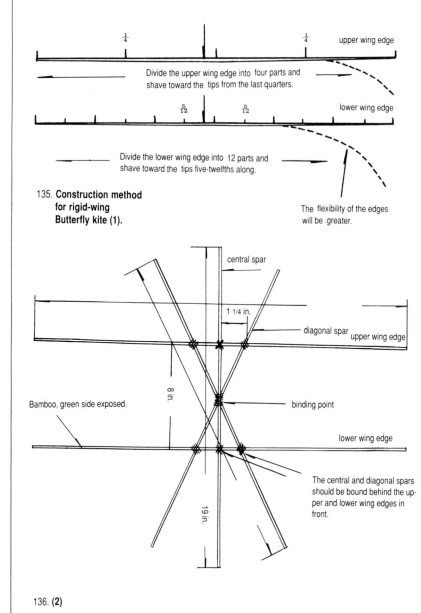

Divide the upper wing edge into four parts and shave toward the tips from the last quarters.

upper wing edge

lower wing edge

Divide the lower wing edge into 12 parts and shave toward the tips five-twelfths along.

135. **Construction method for rigid-wing Butterfly kite (1).**

The flexibility of the edges will be greater.

central spar

1 1/4 in.

diagonal spar

upper wing edge

Bamboo, green side exposed.

binding point

lower wing edge

8 in.

19 in.

The central and diagonal spars should be bound behind the upper and lower wing edges in front.

136. **(2)**

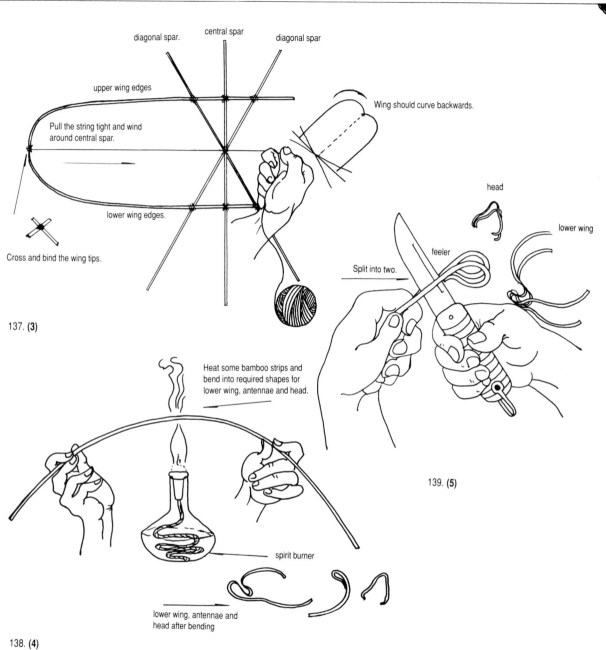

diagonal spar.   central spar   diagonal spar

upper wing edges

Pull the string tight and wind
around central spar.

Wing should curve backwards.

lower wing edges.

Cross and bind the wing tips.

137. **(3)**

head

lower wing

feeler

Split into two.

139. **(5)**

Heat some bamboo strips and
bend into required shapes for
lower wing, antennae and head.

spirit burner

lower wing, antennae and
head after bending

138. **(4)**

7)Glue on the cover. First put glue on the front and back of the main wings. The main wing has a fixed shape because of the binding method and the ends of the wings should curve backwards. The distance along the string from wing tip to wing tip is the longest part of the kite. To glue the cover as smoothly as possible to the upper wing, make a nick at either end of the paper. Push the paper forward from the back of the kite. This will mean that the frame is behind the paper and the towline in front. Apply the paste to the frame and pull the paper toward each corner, to help keep it flat. The margins can be trimmed. The cover for the head, antennae and the lesser wing should be glued flat in this way (fig.141).

8) Paint a butterfly design on the cover. Choose your own colors (fig. 142).

9) Lastly, attach the bridle as shown in fig. 143. Tie the three strings together about 2 1/2" away from the frame to form the bridle (fig.143).

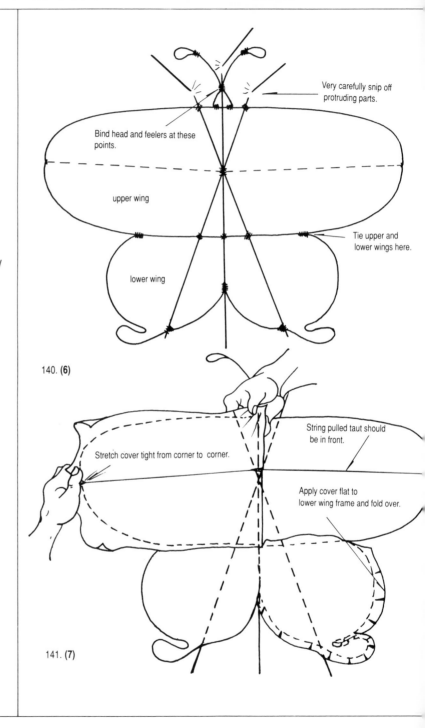

Very carefully snip off protruding parts.

Bind head and feelers at these points.

upper wing

Tie upper and lower wings here.

lower wing

140. **(6)**

String pulled taut should be in front.

Stretch cover tight from corner to corner.

Apply cover flat to lower wing frame and fold over.

141. **(7)**

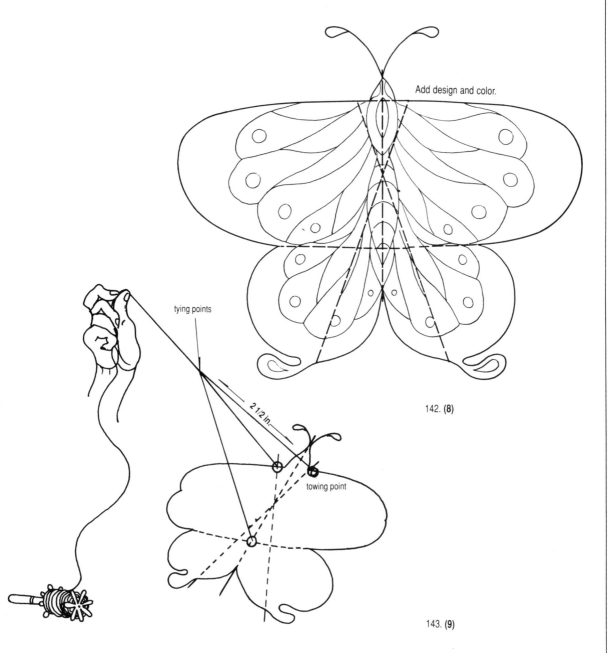

Add design and color.

tying points

2 1/2 in.

towing point

142. **(8)**

143. **(9)**

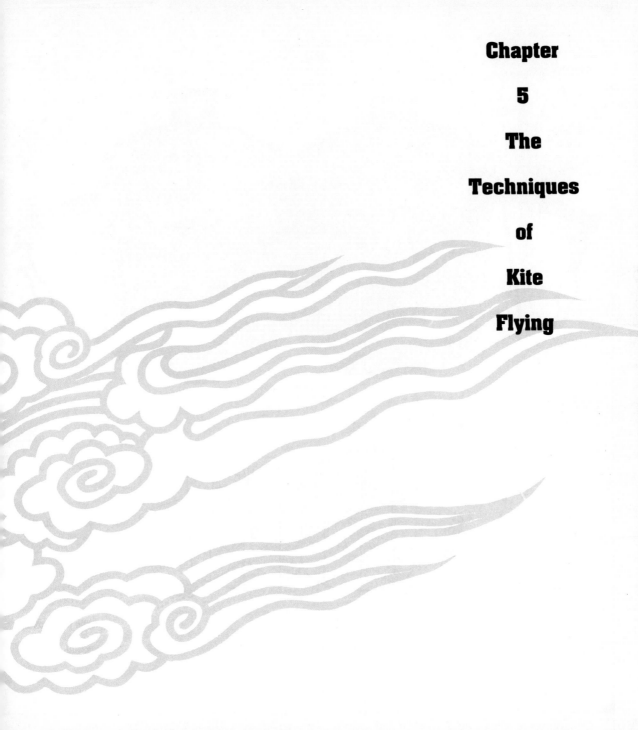

Chapter 5 The Techniques of Kite Flying

To master the skills of kite flying, it is necessary to understand some principles of aerodynamics and characteristics of kites in relation to them. In general, there are four significant factors: 1) a kite cannot move by itself; 2) it needs air currents to move; 3) it needs a towline; 4) it needs to be facing the wind.

In simplest terms, a kite stays in the air because the weight of the kite and an air current counter each other's force. A kite rises on a windy day because the wind's force is stronger than gravity pulling the kite down. On a windless day a kite can still be flown by pulling quickly in one direction because the kite and the air will be creating counter-forces. The kite's resistance to the air current will cause it to fly.

But the principles of aerodynamics are also involved. The kite has several different faces. According to the size, tension, direction, angle and differences in distance and position from the point of pull (usually in the kite's center) of these faces, there are many differences in the degree of wind resistance. If the surface area is large and lacks tension and if each face has a vertical angle of attack, then there will be greater wind resistance. On the other hand, if the surface area is small and tight and if each face has a diagonal angle of attack, then there will be little wind resistance.

When the air current strikes the front of the kite, the current's speed decreases, but the pressure it exerts increases. This causes the air to push strongly on the front surface and flow around the two sides of the kite. After passing around the sides, the air contracts and continues to flow behind the kite. In other words, when the air current exerts a definite pressure against the kite, it will divide into several streams that pass around the kite to meet again immediately behind it. This rush of air creates a low pressure area behind the kite (fig. 144). This difference in air pressure between the front and the back of the kite is actually what keeps the kite rising. The stronger force of air on the front of the kite enables wind to push the kite into the low-pressure "vacuum" created behind the kite. Thus, there is both a lifting force and a counterforce (fig. 144).

When a kite is in the air there are four different forces counterbalancing each other to keep it aloft: the lift counterbalances the pull of gravity while the pushing pressure of the wind against the kite is counterbalanced by the pull of the towline. The force of the wind creates the lift and the push while the pull comes from the kite flier. Only the gravitational force comes from the kite itself (figs. 145–146).

However, an understanding of the principles of aerodynamics does not guarantee an immediate grasp of kite-flying. Because of the many different kinds of kites, certain problems must be considered, such as which points on the kite body are strong enough to attach the towline to and how well the kite will fly in specific conditions.

Two other important points are: 1) the force resulting from the air current is equal to the pressure that the towline is able to take, and 2) because the kite is restricted by the pull of the string, different strengths of string should be used for different kites. For centipede kites, strings of varying strengths should be used for the front, middle and rear sections, with stronger string in front and progressively lighter string for the following sections.

Even if the frame design is carefully worked out, the kite will fly badly or not at all if the towline has been attached to the wrong points. The positioning of the towline and bridle and its length and angle are all vitally important. The towline should be attached at the points on the kite which will be strongest when under pressure, or the kite simply will not fly (fig. 147). The towing point should be above the center of the kite to insure that the kite's natural gravity will be even when flying and being pulled. The parts of the frame in contact with the bridle and the surfaces near these areas are where the kite is resistant to the air current. These are the main tying points. Where the air current encounters resistance, it moves to the two sides and down, and these are the subordinate tying points. The central spar or corresponding two points on those decorative parts which take up a large

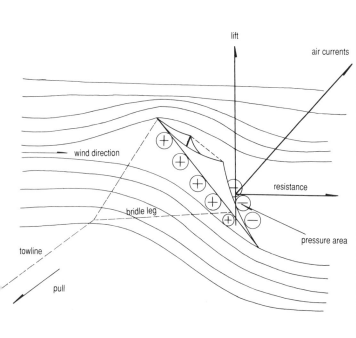

lift

air currents

wind direction

bridle leg

resistance

pressure area

towline

pull

144. **How the kite flies.**

145. **Landing a multi-layered kite.**

146. **Flying a Swallow.**

area of the kite's surface are also important points.

There are many different bridle arrangements, varying from one leg to several. For example, the main tying points of kites with long tails must be moved upward to counterbalance the drag of the tail. If the main tying points are moved upward, the angle of the kite to the wind will be greater, and as the air currents flow over the kite's surface, they will overcome the kite's natural gravity and the tail will then function solely as stabilizer. Similarly, several adjustments must be made to the asterisk-frame human figure kite before flying. Because many parts of

the design are not absolutely symmetrical, the main tying points should be moved from the top or bottom parts of the kite body toward the decorative parts.

The positioning and methods for attaching one to several leg bridles are as follows.

1) One-leg bridle. The Eagle (flexible-wing type) and the Gate-lantern (three dimensional type, use one-leg bridles. The Eagle kite is basically triangular. The wind resistance area of the two wings is comparatively small and is only single-layered. The head and tail are stabilizers. The string should be attached about one-third down from

the head (fig. 149). Each cylinder of the three dimensional tube-shaped Gate-lantern kite is a complete body and there are no accessories, so the string may be attached to any major frame part.

2) Two-leg bridle. The Umbrella kite requires a two-leg bridle. The guiding point and strongest part of this kite is the central spar. The V-shaped crossing pieces are the supports and the small triangular area between them is the main area of wind resistance. The rest of the area of the upper part helps lift it. The rectangular lower part acts mainly as a stabilizer. Two strings should be attached, one to the apex of the upper part at the end of the central spar, and the other to the central spar between the upper and lower parts. The two strings should then be tied together at the towing point (fig. 150).

3) Three-leg bridle. The Butterfly (flexible-wing type) and the rigid square-frame kite take a three-leg bridle. Each wing of the Butterfly may be considered a separate part. When flying, the two wings bend backwards. The upper wings and the abdomen form the strongest part of the body and move the main parts. Two lines should be attached to the two main points where the two upper wings meet the body, and the third line should be attached on the lower abdomen where the two lower wings meet. Then the three lines should be tied together at the towing point (fig. 147).

The rigid square-frame kite has a strong body made up of a single square surface which remains flat when flying. Two strings should be attached respectively at the two points where the upper horizontal spar crosses the two vertical supporting spars. The third string should be tied at the point where the vertical central spar crosses the lower horizontal spar. They should meet at the towing point (fig. 151).

4) Four-leg bridle. Because of its shape, the Flower Basket kite requires a four-leg bridle for greater flying control. Two strings should be attached to the points where the two wings meet the body; one string

should be attached to the lower edge of the wings where it meets the central spar; and the fourth string should be tied to the top part of the kite in the center so that this comparatively large area can be controlled. Without this fourth string, the kite will not fly. The four strings should meet at the towing point (fig. 152).

5) Five-leg bridle. The Catfish (rigid-wing) uses a five-leg bridle for stability. Three strings are attached to the upper and lower edges of the wings in the same way as the flower basket above. However, the decorative part above the upper edge of the wing needs two strings because the two feelers protrude so far. Without these strings, the kite would either be unable to fly or would veer erratically from side to side (fig. 153).

6) Bridles with six legs or more. The number of strings and their correct attachment depends on the different forms and sizes of the kites. Because they are multi-layered, each rigid wing has an important function and the kite is strung together following the main and subsidiary tying points of each wing edge (plate 23).

Air currents constantly vary according to the nature of the environment, whether it be ocean, grassland, mountain, valley or forest. When these air currents encounter solid bodies, their speed and direction will change, producing upward, downward or spiraling

currents. Therefore, the flight of the kite is always highly variable. For example, the string of the kite will be taut when flying from a high hill; the kite will fly low on cloudy days; and in hills it will move in differing directions (figs. 154–156).

Before flying a kite, carefully check the environment and note the wind direction and speed. Because of different strength and resistance, a specific kite is best suited for a specific wind speed.

Here are some basic methods for flying three different kites.

1) The Sand Swallow. On launching, the Sand Swallow will waver from side to side but will remain stable once up in the air. This is because the lower air currents are less stable and slower than those at higher altitudes. The string should be released slowly in order to allow the kite to rise gently through the lower air currents into the faster currents above.

Most of the sand swallow's weight is concentrated in the center. To launch this kite, two or three helpers are required, in addition to a strong wind. The first person holds the kite face downwards; the second stands at a distance of 15 yards from the first and holds the string up, while a third person stands another 30 yards away and controls the string. The three people should release the string in relay fashion, starting with the kite.

2) The Catfish. The tail of this kite is very long and in order to

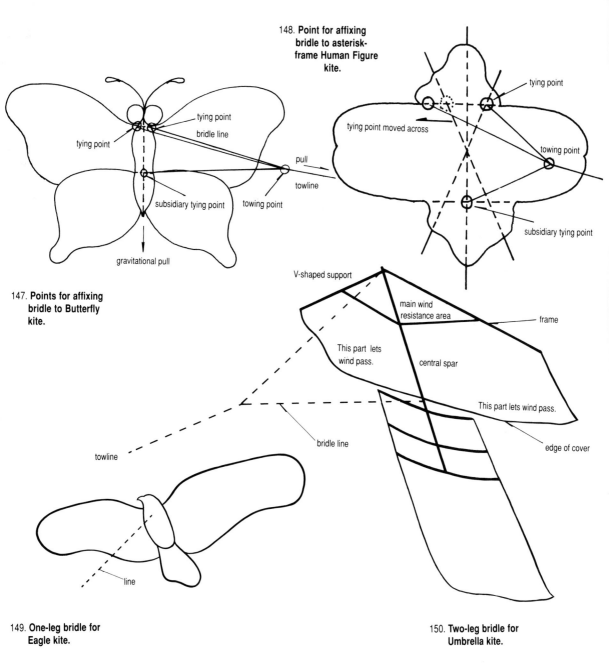

148. **Point for affixing bridle to asterisk-frame Human Figure kite.**

tying point

tying point moved across

towing point

subsidiary tying point

tying point

tying point

bridle line

tying point

pull

towline

subsidiary tying point

towing point

gravitational pull

147. **Points for affixing bridle to Butterfly kite.**

V-shaped support

main wind resistance area

frame

This part lets wind pass.

central spar

This part lets wind pass.

bridle line

edge of cover

towline

line

149. **One-leg bridle for Eagle kite.**

150. **Two-leg bridle for Umbrella kite.**

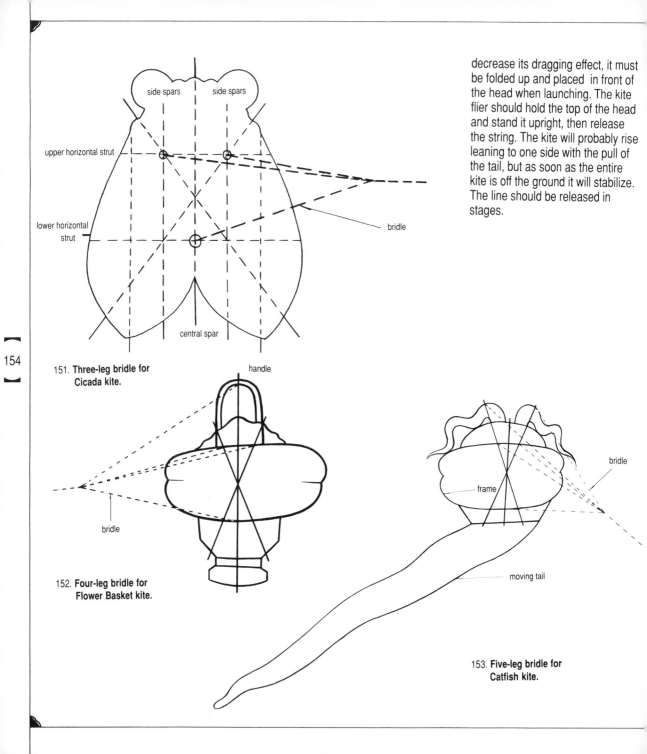

decrease its dragging effect, it must be folded up and placed in front of the head when launching. The kite flier should hold the top of the head and stand it upright, then release the string. The kite will probably rise leaning to one side with the pull of the tail, but as soon as the entire kite is off the ground it will stabilize. The line should be released in stages.

side spars

side spars

upper horizontal strut

lower horizontal strut

bridle

central spar

151. **Three-leg bridle for Cicada kite.**

handle

bridle

152. **Four-leg bridle for Flower Basket kite.**

frame

bridle

moving tail

153. **Five-leg bridle for Catfish kite.**

3) *The Centipede*. There are two kinds of centipede kites, one with a comparatively short tail with about thirty layers, the other with thirty to several hundred layers. Each has a different flying method. The shorter centipede kite only needs two fliers, one to lift the kite and the other to hold the towline and give it continuous shakes to send ripples down the line. The line should be gradually let out while the person holding the kite should lift and launch it. The method of launching the long-tailed centipede kite is the same, except that the longer the kite, the more assistants will be required. For example, a 40-yard kite with a hundred layers can require as many as six people to launch successfully (fig. 160).

Table showing effects of different winds on land.
Windscale Windspeed (yds/second) Effects on land

0	0.23 and under	Calm; smoke rises up
1	0.3-1.6	Smoke begins to show wind direction
2	1.7-3.6	Can feel breeze; leaves rustle; some wind current
3	3.7-5.9	Leaves and small branches move; flags unfurl a little
4	6.0-8.6	Dust and paper fly up; small branches wave
5	8.7-11.7	Small trees bend; small waves on water surfaces
6	11.8-15.0	Branches of large trees bend; phone wires hum; hard to hold umbrella
7	15.1-18.7	Whole trees bend; walking against wind is difficult
8	18.8-22.6	Small branches break; very difficult walking into wind
9	22.7-26.7	Objects on roofs blown off; some damage to trees
10	26.8 ++	Rarely seen on land; very destructive

155. Kite-flying on a cloudy day.
Altitude will be reduced.

154. Kite-flying from a high point.
The kite string will be pulled taut.

156. Kite-flying in a hilly area.
Kite may change direction abruptly.

b) Kite's flight will be erratic as it encounters winds that change direction according to varying hill heights.

157. Directions of wind according to surroundings:
a) Difficult to fly in a built-up area as wind changes directions frequently.

c) In trees wind will be erratic and sometimes obstructed, making kite-lying difficult here too.

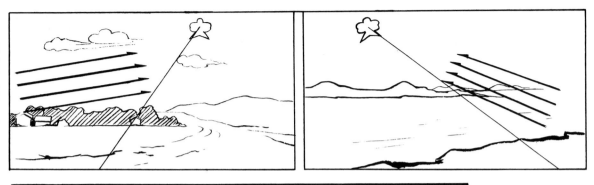

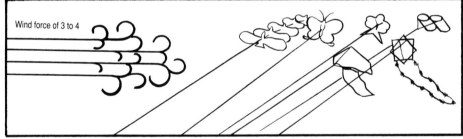

Wind force of 2 to 3

d) In open spaces kite-flying is much easier as air currents will maintain consistent force and direction.

e) The seaside is a good place to fly kites.

Wind force of 3 to 4

158. Choosing kite style to fit the wind:

Wind force of 2 to 3: use soft-flap, flexible-wing and rigid-wing of various sizes.

Wind force of 3 to 4: use medium-sized flexible-wing, rigid-wing, flexible square-frame and umbrella kites; also small to medium-sized three-dimensional and multi-layered.

Wind force of 4 to 6: large and medium-sized, rigid square-frame and multi-layered. Accessories such as gong and drum, hummers and whistles may be attached.

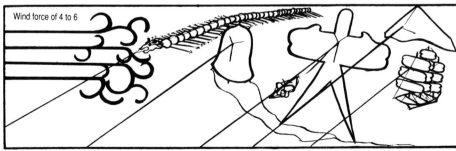

Wind force of 4 to 6

159. **Best angle for flying a kite.** The kite should be maintained between 45°to 90° to the ground.

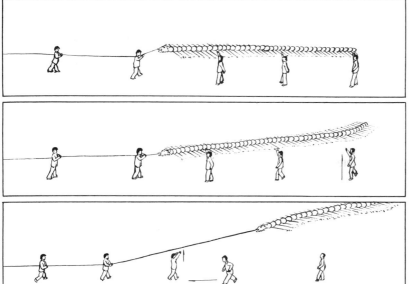

160. **Flying Dragon-headed Centipede kites of thirty layers or over:**

a) Each person stands at a distance of 10 yards from the other, with three handling kite and two holding string.

b) Person at end should launch his or her section first, with two others following in succession.

c) After launching, each person should lift up his or her section of the string and release in sequence.

This is the first book-length guide to the art and craft of Chinese kite-making as practiced by the Ha family, famed kite-makers for four generations. Here, in their own words, the Has reveal the artistic principles and construction techniques of their magnificent kites.

For over a hundred years, the Has have been developing the art and craft of kite-making. Ever since their kites were presented to the Qing emperor in the nineteenth century, their skills have been recognized, and their kites have won international accolades as far back as 1915, when they took a prize at the Panama International Fair. In 1982, Ha Kuiming (third generation kite-maker and co-author) was invited to France to lecture and demonstrate his art. In the two following years, his son and co-author, Ha Yiqi, toured the United States to demonstrate both kite construction and flying.

The Has have perfected all six major elements of kites: binding, gluing, decorating, flying, understanding the relationship between wind and kite, and line control. They have also transformed a traditional folk craft into a superb art. Their kites have become noted for framework, skillful designs, magnificent decoration and improved flying performance.

This book presents in detail the complete kite-making process and the special techniques of construction and design. With color illustrations of over 80 rare and superb kites from the Ha collection, plus over 160 figures and diagrams with explanatory notes showing all kite techniques, the Has have created both a fine art album and a readable how-to book.

Ha Kuiming.

Born in 1917, Ha Kuiming is a lifelong Beijing resident. At the age of ten, he began to learn kite-making from his father, and took over the family's kite company at age eighteen. His half century of experience has helped establish the Has among the world's foremost kite-makers. His kites have been exhibited at home and abroad as his international reputation has grown. In 1982 he was invited to lecture on kites at the Chinese Kite Exhibition held in France. He serves as technical advisor to the Beijing Kite Company and is a member of the Arts and Crafts Institute and president of the Beijing Kite Association.

Ha Yiqi.

Born in 1954, Ha Yiqi was initiated into the kite tradition by his father, Ha Kuiming, at age ten. He expanded his artistic approach to kites by studying traditional Chinese painting and oil painting. In 1982, his Phoenix-Butterfly kite took a second prize at the Beijing Arts and Crafts Exhibition. In 1983, he was invited to participate in the Chinese Kite Exhibition and China Kite Week in the United States, and in the same year took a prize at the International Kite Festival in California. In 1984, he demonstrated kite-making and flying at the Chinese Traditional Craft Exhibition held at the American Pacific Science Center. He is assistant manager of the Beijing Folk Art Company and manager of Research and Development of the Beijing Kite Company